Parental Advisory

Parental Advisory

How to Protect Your Family in the Digital Age of Identity Theft and Data Breaches

David Derigiotis, CIPP/US

ISBN: 978-1-68913-731-7

Your privacy isn't dead. It's only been resting.

About the Book

CHILDREN TODAY ARE GROWING UP in the middle of a digital war where information is collected, sold, and scraped at every turn, and another new headline reveals a security incident from a business that failed to protect our data.

Cyberattacks have exposed every sensitive detail imaginable, leaving behind a threat of identity theft that will last a lifetime. This modern-day epidemic of lost privacy is being experienced by people at a younger age, and it feels as if nothing can be done to protect our children. Every detail is documented, shared, and preserved forever online and available to any data broker, criminal, or researcher who knows how to find it. This frustration has left people wondering how we made it to this point and whether anything can be done.

But before you give up all hope, know that there is help. You can gain the advantage in an online world and achieve greater privacy and cybersecurity within your home. You can teach your children to use the internet smarter and more anonymously.

In this powerful and eye-opening view into our digital insecurities, the author will walk you through a variety of techniques used to uncover privacy weak spots and provide the necessary solutions throughout the entire process. Specific data breaches and privacy mishaps experienced by companies will be discussed along the way and why they should matter to you.

If you have children who play video games online, use a smartphone or tablet, or you thought privacy was impossible to achieve, this book is for you. If you are looking for ways to educate your family on safe cyber practices and build lifelong good habits, this book is for you.

The unique perspective of the author will allow you to look through the eyes of an adversary while preparing you to live as a privacy professional. Cybercrime is a lucrative business for those involved. Don't allow your family to be a profitable investment for criminals.

This is a Parental Advisory: understand your vulnerabilities, make the necessary changes, and reduce your cyber insecurities. Your privacy isn't dead. It's only been resting. Time to wake up.

Table of Contents

Talking about Practice

IN A WORLD OF CYBERCRIME, most people do not need to worry about being the target of a sophisticated hacking group or falling prey to an unknown software vulnerability on a smartphone. The most significant threats to our home, children, and family come from opportunistic criminals who are experts in deception and know how to take full advantage of our oversharing ways and inability to use technology securely. Criminals are skilled and well trained in their craft and take full advantage of our lack of preparation and understanding in safe cyber and privacy practices.

Training and preparation are needed for so many of the things we do in life, especially if a particular task is to be done well. If you play sports, then you understand it is important to practice, recognize the rules, master techniques, and learn how the offense and defense manage a variety of game play situations. In the academic world, passing classes in school requires studying, completing homework, reading, and demonstrating you comprehend the content through effective test taking and positive results. Simply show-ing up on the day of a game or exam and expecting to attain a positive outcome will not be possible if the proper time was not dedicated to the task before-hand. This is the critical mistake so many make when it comes to life in the online world. Not enough people take the time to understand the technology that is placed in our hands or how our information is abused and shared between the companies we so readily pro-vide it to.

A tablet, gaming system, or other connected de-vice is placed in front of our youngest users with little to no guidance given on how it should be used safely and securely on the internet. Technology is ending up in the hands of our children at a younger and younger age these days. A colleague of mine had told me of the time his three-year-old daughter was given a physi-cal picture frame containing a single family photo to observe. She sat there confused as she swiped across the glass of the frame with her finger, expecting the picture to move off the screen and another to appear right behind it. This is an experience only a smartphone or tablet screen can offer and highlights just how early technology is being introduced to our youngest mem-bers of society.

Children today are growing up in a digitally con-nected world unlike anything their own parents expe-rienced as kids. If we as parents or guardians are not properly equipped to deal with using technology safe-ly or don't understand how to maintain greater privacy when engaging on social media platforms or with organizations that collect and share our personal information, how in the world can we expect our children to do so responsibly? The lure of the convenience factor, cool new features offered by the latest products, and the ease of use allows us to adopt technology of all types into our lives like never before. The question that must be asked is what will the tradeoff be for all of the perceived benefits? What are we giving up?

The answer is our privacy and cyber safety if we are not thoughtful about our actions online. The connectivity, access to information, people, data, and speed at which we can move from one part of the world to another through the use of computers is astonishing. There is, however, another side of the coin that we must consider. The easy access and connectivity come with a caution sign many fail to read and a parental advisory that must be observed, especially when dealing with children. Most people are not properly prepared or equipped to deal with the personal threats to cybersecurity and privacy that come with such connectivity and access. Most of us are vulnerable in ways we never knew existed, and it will only be a matter of time until identity theft or fraud come knocking at the door.

There are many simple yet effective things that can be done to protect ourselves in this overexposed and connected age we are all living in. This book was written with the family in mind but can serve as a guide for people of all ages and technical abilities. Discussed throughout the following chapters are a variety of cyber and privacy best practices that will prove useful for anyone living in the digital world. Unless you are completely disconnected from the grid, this will apply to most of us. The strategies and tips suggested can be implemented gradually and might be the difference between having to deal with identity theft or fraud and remaining secure and anonymous. While you read, do not feel compelled to make each change immediately as additional insight and solutions will be further unpacked throughout the book. Some of the tips provided in earlier chapters are best paired with concepts that are discussed later. For the parent looking to educate children in a world of constant corporate privacy and security mishaps, this book was written for you. This roadmap will equip the reader with an ability to minimize their digital footprint and operate more securely online.

You can and should be an active player in the online world, but the burden is on you to do so responsibly. The obligation of protecting your privacy and security cannot rest solely on the shoulders of government or private corporations. Countless companies have reminded us time and time again that they are not capable of securing our information, some more than others. With prior headlines surrounding Facebook storing hundreds of millions of user passwords in plaintext over the course of several years, telecom companies such as AT&T, T-Mobile, and Sprint selling customers' real-time location data to third parties, some of which were bounty hunters, Starwood hotels exposing passport and credit card numbers, or the historic Equifax breach compromising the personal information of 143 million people, it may seem like nothing about us has been left to the imagination. But even with all of these security incidents and plenty more that will certainly follow, this should not be an excuse to throw in the towel or be the reason we fail to train the next generation of technology users. We can be more secure online and take back our privacy with a little bit of work. In some cases it may be a lot of work. As they say, old habits die hard, and this may require some significant behavioral changes around how you have been operating in the digital world for years now. Congratulations to you for taking the first step by reading this far. This is where some time and energy have to be spent on your part. If you want to achieve greater privacy, you have to be intentional. This book will help you to do that.

Highlighted throughout the chapters will be a number of offensive and defensive techniques that will serve two purposes. One, a strong offense will allow you to think like an attacker and see through the eyes of an adversary. This perspective will allow you to uncover the vulnerabilities a social engineer might look for in a target and reduce those exposures for you and your family. A solid offense will also allow you to proactively investigate the privacy and security holes in your game before someone else does and fix them.

Second, the defensive side of the coin will allow you to harden the personal security posture of you and your family. A good defense can prevent an attacker from being able to take advantage of you. If you are too hard of a target, they will move on to the next person.

The end goal of bringing both of these methods together will be to establish a safer online environment for your household and provide the training and knowledge needed to move freely and privately in a digital world.

Try not to become overwhelmed with all of the cleanup work that may need to be done for you and your family online. All of your information was not accumulated and shared overnight, and it will not be removed or changed overnight either. This is a process and will help develop strong privacy and security habits for those within the household that can be carried on for a lifetime. Some of the methods and tactics discussed in this book will change over time, as technology is always evolving, but one point I hope to drive home with this approach is to create a privacy-focused mind-set.

Moving forward, I hope you will question why an organization needs your information and think carefully before you provide it. What are the business purposes for collecting this data, and who will it be shared with? What are the risks to my family once it is compromised, and what steps will need to be taken to reduce the likelihood of fraud or identity theft? As you progress throughout the chapters, these questions will all be addressed.

So buckle up and get ready, as you are about to be in for an eye-opening ride. On the other end of this book is a safer and more digitally secure future for you and your young technology users. Privacy isn't dead, it's only been resting. Time to wake up.

CHAPTER 1

What Is Personal and Sensitive Information?

WHAT MAY SEEM AS INSIGNIFICANT information for many people or organizations can be used as a starting point to unlock other, more identifying details surrounding an individual. The data used at the starting line of an information-gathering race does not have to involve Social Security numbers, banking details, or passwords but rather information we effortlessly give away through the course of normal conversations with strangers or maybe even have posted somewhere within our social media profiles. We must be mindful of the information that is freely given away, as it can have unintended privacy or security consequences. You never know who may come across your profile or who might be actively searching for it. This becomes more of a concern when the profile belongs to a minor, and we will come back to this.

What Is PII?

What is considered sensitive and personally identifiable information (PII) in the United States can mean different things depending on whom you ask. Our laws and regulations are a patchwork of federal, state, and professional body guidelines that vary based upon the industry a business operates within or the type of information that is collected and processed.

For example, the healthcare industry has to abide by the federally mandated Health Insurance Portability and Accountability Act (HIPAA). This regulation focuses on medical records, health status, provision of health, and will extend to any organization that assists in the processing of medical billing, coding, or supporting services for what are called covered entities (healthcare provider, health plan, or healthcare clearinghouse). Here, health-related information is considered sensitive, and for that reason it is protected.

The financial services industry must adhere to the Gramm-Leach Bliley Act (GLBA), which deals with information pertaining to loans, financial or investment advice, or insurance. Organizations are required to explain their information-sharing practices to their customers and to properly protect this sensitive data.

Professional body/self-regulating organizations such as the Payment Card Industry Data Security Standards (PCI-DSS) oversee any organization that accepts, transmits, or stores cardholder data for any of the five US card associations. The card associations are made up of Visa, MasterCard, Discover, American

Express, and JCB International. In this case, payment card data is sensitive.

In addition to these identifiers, each state also individually defines what is considered sensitive information as well. For example, the state of California defines PII as follows within their data breach notification law:

> (A) An individual's first name or first initial and his or her last name in combination with any one or more of the following data elements, when either the name or the data elements are not encrypted:
>
> (1) Social Security number; (2) driver's license number or California identification card number; (3) account number, credit, or debit card number, in combination with any required security code, access code, or password that would permit access to an individual's financial account; (4) medical information; (5) health insurance information; (6) information or data collected through the use or operation of an automated license plate recognition system, as defined in Section 1798.90.5.

(B) A username or email address in combination with a password or security question and answer that would permit access to an online account.

Medical Information-Specific Statute

For clinics, health facilities, home health agencies, and hospices licensed pursuant to sections 1204, 1250, 1725, or 1745 of the Cal. Health and Safety Code, the Medical Information Breach Notification statute may apply. The statute applies to patients' medical information. "Medical information" means any individually identifiable information, in electronic or physical form, in possession of or derived from a provider of health care, health care service plan, pharmaceutical company, or contractor regarding a patient's medical history, mental or physical condition, or treatment. "Individually identifiable" means that the medical information includes or contains any element of personal identifying information sufficient to allow identification of the individual, such as the patient's name, address, electronic mail address, telephone number, or Social Security number, or other

> information that, alone or in combina-
> tion with other publicly available infor-
> mation, reveals the individual's identity.

As you can see in the case of California state law, there are particular items that have to be involved together in order to trigger notification requirements by a business. This is a common factor for all of the state data breach notification laws. For example, if a security incident at a business involved a customer's first and last name combined with a Social Security number or an email address along with a password and this information was not encrypted, a customer would have to be notified of this incident. These items coupled together would raise the possibility of future harm, such as identity theft or fraud for those who had their information compromised. However, if it were only the customer's name and email address or name and phone number, no notification would be required by law.

The question I want you to ask is: What possible harm could come from sharing or exposing such simple pieces of information like an email address? How many different nonessential services and critical activities such as banking, investments, and insurance are being tied to a single email account? We give our name and email contact to countless business, websites, and social media platforms without thinking twice. It is time we reconsider what is viewed as sensitive and understand the possible harm that could come from this data if and when it falls into the wrong hands or becomes exposed in a breach.

A Community of Investigators

There is an entire community of people dedicated to gathering information from publicly available sources, known as open source intelligence (OSINT). This method of overt gathering is the opposite of covert information gathering and can yield a significant amount of personal details when done strategically. There are many different websites and tools that can be utilized completely free of charge for legitimate and appropriate purposes or with bad and harmful intentions, depending on the motive of the seeker. Will the information collected be used to help solve a cyberbullying case where a perpetrator is unmasked through various cyber investigation practices, or will it be used to carry out a social engineering attack against a minor who was oversharing online and didn't realize the implications? I have seen cyberstalking and bullying in full effect, and it is both heartbreaking and troubling. An eye-opening amount of personal information is floating around online and fully accessible to those who know where to find it, and there are always people looking. Intentionally exposing too much information and being unaware of the various tactics that can be used against you will expose you to possible harm.

In the business world, I try and help organizations uncover their cyber and privacy weak spots and establish a more resilient cyber- and privacy-focused posture. I do much of this through conferences and presentations, where I walk the audience through a variety of ways they can be tricked or deceived by using information that is readily available. This information may seem harmless at first but can be used as the critical bait needed to gain so much more. Reducing organizational risk is a process that is done through self-reflection/analysis, anticipation of threats, and preparation. The same will be true for the individual and family. Having a clear understanding of your digital footprint and how it could be used against you, reducing your risk where possible, and preparing for anticipated scams or attacks will allow your family to raise the digital wall for greater protection. Knowing the tactics used by the offensive will allow you to plan for a better defense.

All of our information carries a varying degree of sensitivity and can be used in a variety of ways depending on the adversary's motive. Payment card data can be used for fraud, allowing an attacker to order items online or purchase gas at the pump under our name. The quick fix is to cancel the card and have the bank reissue a new one immediately, removing that threat. Social Security numbers present a much bigger problem, as this information can be used to conduct nearly any identity theft tactic desired. Filing tax returns, taking out new loans, having medical treatment, and even building a criminal record can all be done fraudulently and under a victim's name if you know their Social

Security number. Unfortunately, this threat will stick with you for the rest of your life once this information is in the open. The reality of the situation is that for nearly all of us it has been exposed. Although the fix isn't as easy as getting a new payment card issued, I will talk about what a credit freeze can do to help reduce the risk of identity theft in chapter 10.

What Is in a Name and Email Address?

Right now we will focus on two very common pieces of information—your name and email address. They seem so harmless, and these basic identifiers have been swept up in data breach after data breach over the years with such frequency that people have become numb to the latest company making headlines by announcing another security incident. In November 2018 Amazon informed customers that their names and email addresses were exposed in what was called a technical error in their website. In January 2019 a massive data breach list of eight hundred million email addresses and passwords surfaced online, known as "Collection #1." This list was compiled from several separate data breaches that have occurred over the years and was ultimately assembled into one large data set. In 2013 and 2014 Yahoo suffered two separate attacks that resulted in all three billion users being compromised.

Again, we are talking about basic identifiers, not what has traditionally been thought of as sensitive data. The Europeans may have it right in how they define personal data under their sweeping privacy law known as the General Data Protection Regulation (GDPR). This landmark privacy rule was adopted in April 2016 and was made effective in May 2018.

Under Article 4 (the regulation has ninety-nine articles and includes more than thirty thousand words detailing the rules and procedures for organizations to follow as it relates to data collection, security, and consumer privacy rights) *personal data* is defined as:

> Any information relating to an identified or identifiable natural person ("data subject"); an identifiable natural person is one who can be identified, directly or indirectly, in particular by reference to an identifier such as a name, an identification number, location data, an online identifier or to one or more factors specific to the physical, physiological, genetic, mental, economic, cultural or social identity of that natural person.

This definition is incredibly broad and will encompass nearly any piece of information that can uncover even the smallest aspect of an individual's identity; this includes a name and email address. The European government is treating all of this information as sensitive, and I think it is time we do too.

In addition to the state data breach notification law, California has also passed its own privacy-focused law called the California Consumer Privacy Act (CCPA) and is the first of its kind in the United States. The goal is to give consumers control over how their personal information is used and allow them to stop businesses from selling that information. I share with you these two privacy laws, as I want you to rethink what you consider sensitive information to be for you and your family. Under the CCPA, personal information is defined as:

> information that identifies, relates to, describes, references, is capable of being associated with, or could reasonably be linked, directly or indirectly, with a particular consumer or device, including, but not limited to:
>
> (1) Identifiers such as a real name, alias, postal address, unique identifier, internet protocol address, electronic mail address, account name, Social Security number, driver's license number, passport number, or other similar identifiers;
>
> (2) Any categories of personal information enumerated in Civil Code 1798.80 et. seq; (For those who are interested, personal information under this code

is defined as: "Personal information" means any information that identifies, relates to, describes, or is capable of being associated with, a particular individual, including, but not limited to, his or her name, signature, Social Security number, physical characteristics or description, address, telephone number, passport number, driver's license or state identification card number, insurance policy number, education, employment, employment history, bank account number, credit card number, debit card number, or any other financial information, medical information, or health insurance information. "Personal information" does not include publicly available information that is lawfully made available to the general public from federal, state, or local government records.)

(3) Characteristics of protected classifications under California or federal law;

(4) Commercial information, including records of property, products or services provided, obtained, or considered, or other purchasing or consuming histories or tendencies;

(5) Biometric data;

(6) Internet or other electronic network activity information, including but not limited to, browsing history, search history, and information regarding a consumer's interaction with a website, application, or advertisement;

(7) Geolocation data;

(8) Audio, electronic, visual, thermal, olfactory, or similar information;

(9) Psychometric information;

(10) Professional or employment-related information;

(11) Inferences drawn from any of the information identified above; and

(12) Any of the categories of information set forth in this subdivision as they pertain to the minor children of the consumer.

As outlined above, this definition again is very broad and encompassing, and it certainly includes an individual's name and email address within the scope of personal information. Often, our email address is associated with our first and last name, which can be used to track down other sensitive details such as personal phone numbers, residence, family members, employer, IP address, social media accounts, and more. All of this information is publicly accessible, unfortunately, which is why our names and email addresses are so important. They hold the keys to obtaining a much more robust set of personal details on our lives. They can serve as the breadcrumb trail leading to the whole loaf.

As a test case, I encourage you to experiment with your own name or your child's to see what you can find. Here is where taking an offensive approach can help you plan for a better defense. Open your browser and enter either your name or email address into a couple different search engines. Use the more common search engines such as Google Chrome and Microsoft-owned Bing to see what comes up. I think you will be surprised. This exercise will show just how large your digital footprint might be and how easily accessible your information will be to anyone who is looking.

OSINT tip: When conducting your search, place quotation marks around your email address and/or name ("jwilson@example.com" or "Jeff Wilson"). Doing so will refine the search and instruct the query to pull only those results that display what is in the search exactly. This is a technique OSINT practitioners will use to cut down on unrelated search results. Conduct another search of your name and email addresses together with quotation marks around each to see where this information is appearing online together on the same page. This can be done with other pieces of data, such as your phone number or home address (ex. "Jeff Wilson" "555-555-5555").

In addition to having a first and last name built into the structure of an email address, which gives up your identity, people tend to use only one or two email addresses for everything they do online. With so many different activities being tied back to one communication vehicle (Yahoo, Microsoft, Gmail, etc.), it places you in harm's way considering how many data breaches that have occurred and involved this information. This will especially put your employer at an elevated risk if many of your personal online activities are linked to your work email account. Your email address and other identifiable information is not only available on the dark web but also on a variety of other sites that scrape and accumulate detailed individual profiles available for anyone to access.

Reflect on your own situation for a moment. Despite all of the data breaches you may have been involved in over the years where your name and email addresses were compromised, have you ever stopped using that same email address? How many different sites are you tied to with that single email address?

Banking, investments, your children's school, work? Do you have this email address displayed anywhere online? Social media accounts, a blog, website, maybe a work bio? With this type of dependence on one email address and so many different aspects of our online life tied to it, all it will take is one phishing email to get through to gain access to other critical accounts you control.

It is even easier for the attacker if you are using the same password for multiple sites. No sophisticated hack is needed here when passwords are all the same. Your compromised email address and password that were involved with the retailer you ordered clothes from will be matched to your place of employment if they are exactly the same. It will not be a person manually looking for the match either, as that would require far too much work. Compromised email address and password lists are loaded into a software program that scours the web looking for matches. This entire process is fully automated and efficient. This is why it is so critical not to reuse the same password for multiple online accounts.

Getting back to privacy, let me show you how a full picture can be painted of any individual when starting with a very limited amount of data by using a real-world example:

In April 2019 I presented at a cybersecurity conference at Harrah's Hotel and Casino in New Orleans, LA. As part of the keynote closing session, I was speaking on the use of OSINT techniques and how they can be used for social engineering a target. One brave soul volunteered prior to my presentation, allowing me to demonstrate what could be collected on a person when starting only with a name and email address. I began my investigation by conducting a specific Google search of the volunteer's name and email address ("First and last name" "email address") and found a match with his employer within the search results.

As a sidenote, when I first entered the individual's name and email address into Google Chrome to search for information, far too much information came back that was not relevant or specific to my target. After I searched a second time using the targeted quotation marks around the name and email, much more refined data came back, making the search more fruitful and relevant. This simple but effective search enhancement will cut down on having to scroll through pages upon pages of irrelevant results.

I then went to the employer website and found his bio, work address, and a secondary email address. The secondary email address gave me an indicator of his middle initial. This would be helpful when using a data aggregator/people search site (discussed in chapter 4) to narrow down my search results. Using multiple data aggregator sites, I was able to determine his home address, family members' names and cell phone numbers, my target's home and cell phones' numbers, service provider; I was able to extract voicemail recordings through another tool, obtain a visual of the home residence along with vehicles likely belonging to residents of the home, social media accounts, family photos, and interests discovered through social media accounts. All of this started with just a name and email address!

If your name and email address are involved in a data breach, it should be taken seriously, as it is sensitive information. This should also allow you to reflect on whom you share this information with, especially when it comes to your children. I am setting the stage for you to understand just how serious this has become. We cannot allow "breach fatigue" to blind us into a mindset of giving up and thinking that nothing can be done. Something can be done, but you will have to be intentional with taking back your privacy and enhancing your family's cybersecurity well-being. I will walk through those steps in the coming chapters.

CHAPTER 2

Children's Information Isn't Child's Play

LIKE MANY OTHER CATEGORIES OF data, information about children is being amassed, shared, and collected at a rate many parents may not realize. The statement "data is the new oil" is not an exaggeration. There is big money in data, and children are not exempt from this, although the law tries to help. Not only are these young people oversharing many details of their lives online, but their parents are culprits as well. Details surrounding a child's name, school, location, photos, and interests are all valuable to companies and the accompanying multibillion-dollar advertising industry that fights for targeted placements of products and services. Children's online information is being accumulated by the apps we download, websites we visit, and the connected devices that we use every day.

In schools, children use tablets and iPads to complete work, research a variety of topics, check grades, take photos, and make videos. They come home and play video games not only with the people sitting in the same room but people from around the world as they connect online and interact with strangers hiding behind avatar photos and fake identities. Here is where anonymity is critical for the child, as many times they will be interacting with adults in the gaming world where information should never be shared. For younger children, they may have an internet-connected watch, tablet, or smart toy that allows them to play games, complete puzzles, and send messages and pictures to friends and family members. This all sounds harmless as long as this data is properly protected and the company can guarantee it will never be accessed by outsiders. Of course, no company can make such a claim. In this situation you must assume that data will be accessed at some point by uninvited parties. What information would you be comfortable with if it fell into the hands of a cybercriminal?

In the process of setting up many of these interactive toys, information such as an email address, names of parents and children, age, school, and gender of the child is collected. This is added to voice recordings, messages, pictures, device usage, and other data surrounding use of the device or learning programs as the child plays with the toy. All of this information adds up to become very identifiable and a very comprehensive profile of your child likely before he or she has even reached the age of ten. This is far too much information, and we should assume it will be accessed at some point. How can we be so certain that this will be the case? Because it has already happened before, and I will share a specific example coming up. Properly protecting the information of your children will be a combination of privacy best practices and understanding how certain regulations such as COPPA can work to your advantage.

COPPA. What Is a COPPA?

The Children's Online Privacy Protection Act (COPPA) is a federal regulation that gives parents control over what information online operators such as websites and apps can collect on their children. Only children aged twelve and under fall under the protected cover of COPPA. This regulation is one of the select few that preempts all state laws, meaning that it overrides any state-specific laws that govern children's data for this age range and applies to any business directed to children as well as a general audience website (YouTube as an example) that has actual knowledge they are collecting information from children under the age of thirteen. It is important to know that this regulation exists to give parents rights and control over the data of their children and to place rules around how an organization can go about collecting such data.

> *Notable incident:* In 2018, the FTC settled an agreement with one of the world's largest manufacturers of electronic children's toys, VTech, for allegations that it violated the Children's Online

Privacy Protection Act (COPPA). The following are some of the specific details found within the January 2018 FTC press release:

> "The Commission alleges that the Kid Connect app used with some of VTech's electronic toys collected the personal information of hundreds of thousands of children, and that the company failed to provide direct notice to parents or obtain verifiable consent from parents concerning its information collection practices, as required under the Children's Online Privacy Protection Act (COPPA). In its first children's privacy case involving Internet-connected toys, the FTC also alleges that VTech failed to use reasonable and appropriate data security measures to protect personal information it collected. The company collected personal information from parents on its Learning Lodge Navigator online platform, where the Kid Connect app was available for download, and also through a now-defunct web-based gaming and chat platform called Planet VTech. Before using Kid Connect or Planet VTech, parents were required to register and provide personal information, including their name,

email address, as well as their children's name, date of birth and gender. VTech also collected personal information from children when they used the Kid Connect app.

In November 2015, VTech was informed by a journalist that a hacker accessed its computer network and personal information about consumers, including children who used its Kid Connect app. The FTC also alleges that VTech violated the FTC Act by falsely stating in its privacy policy that most personal information submitted by users through the Learning Lodge and Planet VTech would be encrypted. The company, however, did not encrypt any of this information."

The FTC is responsible for overseeing COPPA and provides the following outline for organizations to comply with on their website:

1. Post a clear and comprehensive privacy policy on the company's website describing its information practices for children's personal information;

2. Provide direct notice to parents and obtain verifiable parental consent, with limited

exceptions, before collecting personal information from children;

3. Give parents the choice of consenting to the
    operator's collection and internal use of a
    child's information but prohibiting the opera-
    tor from disclosing that information to third
    parties;

4. Provide parents access to their child's personal
    information to review and/or have the infor-
    mation deleted;

5. Give parents the opportunity to prevent fur-
    ther use or online collection of a child's per-
    sonal information;

6. Maintain the confidentiality, security, and
    integrity of information they collect from
    children.

It is important to know your privacy rights as parents
and as consumers. Do not allow an organization to
take advantage of you and your children because they
choose to break promises or fail to be less than transparent with their privacy practices. No organization
can ever guarantee that a breach won't occur, but they
should at least be transparent and truthful in how they
go about securing that information. Unfortunately,
companies that promise to protect the information of

our most vulnerable members of society fail to do so again and again. In fact, sometimes they outright lie about their commitment or methods of securing it.

Data that was accessed by criminals in the VTech incident included pictures, messages, and voice recordings of children. Voice recordings can be extremely personal and are considered biometric information, a highly sensitive class of identifiable data. These are all very personal details that can provide an intimate look into a family and should not be trusted to an organization that fails to make privacy and security a priority. In the case mentioned above, VTech agreed to pay $650,000 as part of the settlement with the FTC. This minor slap on the wrist does not make me feel any better about the situation and undervalues the price of the data exposed.

The VTech punishment was small, however, when compared to the record $5.7 million COPPA civil penalty the FTC levied against lip-syncing app Musical.ly, known as TikTok, for collecting personal information from children without parental consent in February 2019. With TikTok, users provided their email address, phone number, name, username, profile picture, as well as a bio to the company. Again, these are very sensitive details when taking privacy into consideration, especially as it relates to children. Too much information is being collected on individuals, and it is starting at an earlier and earlier age. There were some eye-opening violations taking place, as outlined by the FTC, and are worth mentioning in addition to the VTech matter. As outlined in the FTC press release:

> "The operators of Musical.ly—now known as TikTok—knew many children were using the app but they still failed to seek parental consent before collecting names, email addresses, and other personal information from users under the age of 13," said FTC Chairman Joe Simons.

> In addition to creating and sharing videos, the app allowed users to interact with other users by commenting on their videos and sending direct messages. User accounts were public by default, which meant that a child's profile bio, username, picture, and videos could be seen by other users. While the site allowed users to change their default setting from public to private so that only approved users could follow them, users' profile pictures and bios remained public, and users could still send them direct messages, according to the complaint. In fact, as the complaint notes, there have been public reports of adults trying to contact children via the Musical.ly app. In addition, until October 2016, the app included a feature that allowed users to view

other users within a 50-mile radius of their location.

The operators of the Musical.ly app were aware that a significant percentage of users were younger than 13 and received thousands of complaints from parents that their children under 13 had created Musical.ly accounts, according to the FTC's complaint.

The complaint alleges that the operators of the Musical.ly app violated the COPPA Rule by failing to notify parents about the app's collection and use of personal information from users under 13, obtain parental consent before such collection and use, and delete personal information at the request of parents.

This should be a sobering reminder to parents that it is critical to fully understand how our children are interacting on sites, what information is being collected, and what is visible to the public. Just because a site appears to be child friendly does not mean it is safe or compliant with COPPA. Google owned YouTube is a prime example of a general audience platform that attracts a very young viewing audience but has not historically adhered to COPPA rules. Before the dust could settle on the record fine against TikTok mentioned above, YouTube came to an agreement with the FTC in September of 2019 on what is now officially the largest COPPA settlement to date. The agreement orders Google and YouTube to pay $136 million to the FTC and $34 million to New York State for illegally collecting personal information from children without their parents' consent. According to the complaint, YouTube generated millions of dollars by using identifiers, known as cookies, to track and deliver targeted ads to viewers under the age of 13.

Try These Tips

What can those of us who are parents or guardians do in the digital age of social media and connected toys to protect the privacy of our children? First and foremost, do not provide actual identifiable details when creating a user profile for your children. You are not under oath when registering with a site and should not provide any real information as it relates to full name, school, age, or the email address of your child. The risk of providing accurate details far outweighs the rewards. Proving pseudo identities for your children will not put the child at risk if this information is later compromised.

As a method for protecting your family further, a unique and anonymous email address can be created only for the registration and use of a specific product or service. Failing to do so could leave a breadcrumb trail back to the identity of your child and family. I will explain—if anonymous details are provided for your child but your identifiable email address (Jwilson@gmail.com) and real name (Jeff Wilson) are provided during the registration and they later become compromised in a data breach, a direct link will now exist between the actual father's or mother's name/household name and the child. The personal email address and full name of the parent can be used to easily track down the parents' home address through a data aggregation site, and a simple search of social media accounts would likely lead to pictures of the children, where they attend school, ages, and interests.

This scenario offers another supporting factor to both limit what you share on social media and to make sure any social media accounts you do maintain are buttoned up and on the most restrictive privacy settings possible. A public setting for a social media profile will allow someone who is not a direct connection to review all of your photos and posts, creating an unnecessary privacy exposure for you and your family. Creating a unique email address and use of a forwarding email service will be discussed in a later chapter. Make sure a pseudo identity is also provided for the adult. This will help ensure true anonymity and offer no possible leads back to the child.

As mentioned in the VTech data breach, cybercriminals were able to gain access to messages, voice recordings, and images. This can be a lesson learned and a reminder not to leave sensitive content stored in the cloud for long periods of time. This will allow a significant amount of data to swell larger and larger, waiting for a compromise to occur. As the parent, teach your children to purge this information weekly so their aggregation of content remains relatively small. Always make the assumption that it will be accessed at some point by an unauthorized party. The smaller the dataset or sensitive details left available, the better. If there are items you want to keep for the long term, such as photos, back it up locally before deleting and be sure you make this a practice for yourself. This will build good cyber hygiene practices for the future and ensure your child's digital footprint does not balloon out of control.

Back to School

Deleting old content is not relegated solely to connected toys either. Keep in mind the kind of information that is being gathered and accumulated on school-issued tablets used in and out of the classroom setting. The learning environment is very different today than what it was in the 1980s and 1990s. As a matter of fact, it is very different than what it was less than a decade ago. Children who used to lug around heavy backpacks full of books now carry slim tablets capable of accessing the power of the internet. A digital library full of any textbook imaginable is at the fingertips of children and available with the tap of a download button. This convenience factor, however, is not without concern.

In some public schools across the country, tablets are issued to children as early as third grade. These tablets are used both in the classroom and out for a variety of tasks, such as completing homework, researching topics, checking grades, managing assignments, taking pictures and videos, and the list goes on. These tablets become the responsibility of the student and parents for the duration of the time they are assigned to the particular student. For some, this can be for multiple years while the student progresses upward through the school.

The amount of information, much of which can be extremely sensitive, such as a child's innermost thoughts, can be revealed in the search history of a browser or the private data in videos recorded and pictures taken, which will quickly accumulate on these devices. Just think for a moment the amount of data that could be collected over the course of a week, month, or full school year. Much of the data retained on these tablets are specific to school-related assignments, but if your children are anything like mine, there will be plenty of additional information collected during leisure time spent at home or with friends. It is critical to remember these are the property of the school and not your own. Ultimately, you do not own the data.

It is not only the school that has access to this accumulation of information. Schools have vendor partnerships and data-sharing agreements with service providers that are likely very interested in the information collected throughout the course of a year.

Hopefully, these data-sharing agreements are communicated upfront with parents at the start of the school year so there is a clear understanding of what is being collected and who it is being shared with. In addition, vast amounts of information are always vacuumed up by tech companies like Google and Microsoft whenever their services are used, so keep this in mind any time Google Chrome or Microsoft Edge are the browsers of choice. I will cover how to swap these options for a privacy-focused browser such as Firefox in a later chapter. This will allow you to maximize privacy when accessing the web. In order to prevent a data swell on these devices or the cloud environment where the information can be stored, set up a regular timeframe for backing up and saving it to a personal storage if desired and then deleting it. Make sure the content is deleted from both the device and any cloud storage if necessary.

Notable incident: In August 2019, London-based educational software maker Pearson announced they experienced a data breach involving thirteen thousand school and university accounts. The data exposed included student first and last names and, in some cases, date of birth and email addresses. The company provides student monitoring and assessment platforms, which track and evaluate student performance in school.

Some of the data mentioned above may seem harmless, but remember, small amounts of information can be used to put together a much larger puzzle. A school-issued email address will likely contain the school district and/or state the minor attends within the structure of the address. Conducting a simple Google search of that email address will reveal the city, state, and possibly the specific school if it is not apparent from the makeup of the email address itself. From there, carrying out a specific search of the student's last name along with the state, city, or school could locate additional details on the parents, which would lead to identifying the home address, social media accounts, phone numbers, photographs, and more. Again, this is starting only with a name and email address. I will continue to break down how an attacker might view this information and provide the methods used to accumulate additional pieces so that you might change your perspective on how you see it as well. See the offense unfold so you can prepare a better defense.

Online Gaming

For online video game playing, such as the PlayStation Network or Xbox, never allow your child's real name to be displayed as a username or be associated with the actual account. An anonymous and specific email address should be created and used only for gaming, along with a pseudo name or unidentifiable name for online play. The world of gaming has changed dramatically from the Atari and Nintendo days of my childhood. Children are now playing and talking directly with fellow gamers located all over the world. As an example, Fortnite, one of the most popular multiplayer games in the world right now, connects more than two hundred million users worldwide, according to Bloomberg. This phenomenon of a game allows people with a variety of consoles (PlayStation, Xbox, PC, or mobile phone) to connect and play together on a single platform. With this type of reach and mix of gamers ranging from children to adults, it is critical to mask your identity and be mindful of what is shared online. I have seen far too many children playing under the username of their actual identity, which can lead to identifying a child's home address, social media account, and more.

As I previously discussed, a lot can be found with a name. It would be easy for an adversary to pull additional details through what could appear as harmless conversation during gameplay, such as a parent's first name, email address, or where the child goes to school. These bits and pieces of information add up and should never be disclosed.

During one gameplay session, my oldest son told me someone was asking for the name of his parents and where he lived. This is a huge red flag, and he knew better than to disclose that kind of information to a stranger. I recommend that children do not interact online with people they do not know, especially if they are unaware of the privacy risks and are doing so without the supervision of an adult. My children have very limited interaction online with people they have not met in person.

I couldn't end a connected device section of this book without at least mentioning that before you purchase any device, find out what kind of security updates are offered by the manufacturer (if any) and how they can be applied. An update or patch is usually pushed out when new security vulnerabilities are discovered and fixed with the update or if improvements to the user experience are offered. Check the United States Consumer Product Safety Commission website (https://www.cpsc.gov/) for any recalls as well. There have been security vulnerabilities in connected toys previously, such as the Wi-Fi Hello Barbie or the Bluetooth connected Furby doll, allowing them to be hacked and accessed. These toys and their risks seem to get better coverage during the Christmas season, but you should be aware of the risks and informed all year round.

CHAPTER 3

One and Done? Not So Fast

HOW MANY DIFFERENT EMAIL ADDRESSES are you using to move throughout the online world? Using one email address for all of your online activity is risky business considering all the insignificant services getting linked to critical activities. If you find yourself using one email address for important and insignificant activities alike, that is one security strike against you.

The makeup or structure of that email address is another important factor many people overlook. It can be a big hit to your privacy when that email address contains your first and last name. The email address combined with a name are key identifiers that will be used to uncover other, more sensitive details of your life, which I mentioned in the previous chapter. The same email used for online banking or investments should not be the same email you use for Facebook, Twitter, online publications, or ecommerce sites. Doing so increases the likelihood of falling for a phishing attack when that email address ends up compromised through one of the sites you have that address associated with. Using only one or two email addresses for all of your communication and online activities also allows for a larger user profile to be built around all of your online behavior from companies you do business with or access for online services (think Facebook or Google tracking).

As an example, if an email address tied with your first and last name becomes compromised in a data breach from a site that matters little to you (online publication you subscribe to, sandwich shop rewards program, etc.), you would not want that compromise to be used against you in an attack to obtain banking, healthcare, or retirement account credentials, which are clearly much more sensitive and critical. The email address obtained from the security breach at the sandwich shop website could be used to go after your Bank of America account in a phishing attempt—and you may be more likely to fall for it if you use the same email address for both organizations. This is the exact reason why so many successful phishing attempts during the Christmas season all seem to be related to the shipping of items. Criminals are playing the odds when sending out that bogus FedEx or UPS alert to your Gmail or Yahoo account. They are hoping that is an email you have tied to a recent order and that it is an email address you use for everything online. You will easily spot phishing attempts, no matter how perfect or convincing they appear when they end up in your inbox, for something you never use that email account for.

If you segment your email address and apply one specific to banking and do not use it anywhere else, you will be able to better deflect any attempts when you receive a phishing attempt that has come through another email account that you do not have affiliated with that organization. You will easily spot the fake. Email isolation is important. A specific email address for the sandwich shop, one specific to Facebook, another specific for Amazon, and so on. I know it is a lot more work, but the security payoff is well worth it.

Email Structure

For many of us that have been using email for years, the standard setup was to use some combination of your first and last name as the identifier (ex. Johnwilson@ or jwilson@). How many of you are doing this very thing? This is also a very common email structure within many businesses. I think this is a very poor privacy practice on the personal use side, as it provides far too much information about your identity and can be used for additional data-gathering methods by cybercriminals when combined with other pieces of information that are accessible.

We already discussed just how much information can be uncovered about an individual using the email as a starting point. The solution to obtaining greater privacy is to create multiple email addresses that are anonymous in format (ex. Contactme@emailaddress. com) and associated with an alias name. This tactic will provide a dead end back to your actual identity when your email address and "name" have been compromised in a third party data breach. Creating a pseudo name with your email account and using multiple email addresses for specific purposes allows you to isolate your risk and anonymize your identity for greater privacy. Making these needed changes will not only reduce your own exposure, but more importantly, you can educate your children so they can put this best practice to use from the very start.

> *Tip*: Check all of your email addresses in the Have I Been Pwned? (https://haveibeenpwned.com/) data breach compilation list. There will likely be data breaches and companies that have your email address you have never heard of. Never reuse passwords across online accounts.

Business Risks

This portion will pertain to those in the working world who have a company-issued email address. More obvious will be the working mom or dad, but this advice will go a long way for a young person entering the workforce or securing their first internship with a company and being assigned a corporate email address. More responsibility than many realize comes with that company email address. People are the first line of defense as it relates to security, and often it is that human interaction that identifies and stops a phishing attack, or it is the person who inadvertently grants an adversary access to a network-crippling ransomware event through the single click of a link.

On the business side, organizations are likely to have employees using corporate email addresses across a variety of third-party sites. This can include news outlets, social media accounts, trade associations, vendors, clients, and more. The organization can be put at great risk when these third parties experience security incidents of their own, exposing employees' email addresses, passwords, and other identifying information. This exposure provides a breadcrumb trail right back to the company and can easily allow for unauthorized access—especially when employees reuse the same passwords over and over again. Think for a moment: Which third-party sites do you have tied to your corporate email address?

In my role on the cyber and privacy risk management side, it is typical to see employees legitimately using company email addresses for a variety of purposes across third-party sites. There is no way for any organization to guarantee how third parties properly store and secure data. When the business has a formal partnership in place, risk-management tactics can be implemented, such as having a clear understanding of the third party's security practices and requirement of a minimum standard equal to or greater than the organization's, mandate they purchase corporate cyber insurance, and have a hold harmless agreement in place.

With all of this, data breaches will still happen. But what about many of the instances where there is no formal third-party agreement or partnership in place? What about sites being visited by employees where there is no control? On the other side, I have seen many illegitimate uses of corporate email addresses. Some are downright scary. Seeing employee emails tied to infidelity website Ashley Madison has unfortunately been a common occurrence. Not only is this morally wrong, but it places an unnecessary risk on the company where no risk should even exist.

Consider this scenario: an employee of a medical office uses "password" as his password of choice for logging into work each and every morning. Within the office database, he is able to make new appointments for patients, schedule follow-up visits with the doctor, enter details regarding medical insurance and copays, and transfer funds to pay vendors. This employee also uses the same password in combination with his work email to order professional basketball tickets from Ticketfly, an online event locator and ticket distributor. He does this because it is convenient to manage communication from a single email address, and he only has to remember one (bad) password. Later on, it is discovered that Ticketfly experienced a data breach and those people who ordered tickets from the site had their names and email addresses compromised.

In this scenario, which actually did happen as it relates to a breach at Ticketfly, the medical office would be put at significant risk for an account takeover, as the email address and password compromised at Ticketfly are identical to what is used to access the internal network of the medical office. While the danger does exist for an individual to try and manually access the medical network and others one by one looking for matches, this would likely not be the preferred mode of attack. Instead, in the interest of time and opportunity, all of the usernames, names, and passwords would be uploaded into a software program that would scan the entire internet looking for duplicates, which is known as *credential stuffing*. I briefly mentioned this tactic in an earlier chapter. A report would then be furnished with all of the legwork done. An attacker could then simply walk right in through the virtual front door of the medical office, and you would hear in the news months later that a "sophisticated attack" took place. All the while, it was an employee who used a work email for nonwork-related activities and duplicated passwords.

Notable Headlines:
Headline 1: On multiple occasions, parents who have purchased Nest cams have reported incidents where a hacker had gained access to their microphone and baby monitor. Nest, which is owned by Google, is a maker of smart products such as internet-connected thermostats, smoke detectors, cameras, and other security systems. In one particular case, parents were startled during the night when they heard a beeping

noise coming from their baby monitor. Racing to the baby's room to check it out, they found an unknown man's voice broadcasting over the monitor, yelling expletives and then threatening to kidnap their baby. These devices connect online using Wi-Fi and are assessable to outside parties by simple log in and password. Many of these Nest cam security incidents are believed to be from owners of these products using the same exact passwords that were exposed through data breaches of other services.

Headline 2: In July 2019, State Farm, one of the largest insurance and financial service organizations in the United States, was alerted by their security team to a large volume of fraudulent log in attempts to customer accounts. State Farm communicated that an unknown hacker attempted to gain access by using credentials such as usernames and passwords obtained through dark web sites. Again, this did not appear to be a compromise of the State Farm network but rather an attacker taking advantage of a weak spot in personal security practices—password reuse by customers.

I see these things happen all the time across many different corporate environments. This is not necessarily a fault of the employee; it is more of a lack of training and guidance by the employer. There are resources and tools that can be utilized by organizations similar to what consumers can take advantage of with the Have I Been Pwned? website.

Tip: An organization can utilize the BreachAware scanning service (https://breachaware.com/scan) to see what third party data breaches involve employee data (email address, name, DOB, financial information, passwords, etc.). A real-time scan will be made of the company's domain, and a report will be furnished detailing the results. An employer can use this service to be aware of what corporate assets have been involved in third-party breaches, take necessary action such as forcing password resets where needed, and warn employees of potential phishing attacks to come. *Full disclosure*, the organization I work for does have a business relationship with BreachAware. A free, redacted report of a business domain name can still be scanned to see if any compromised credentials are located.

Consider creating multiple junk email accounts, which will allow you to segment your online activity and offer a layer of anonymity when not tied to your actual name. Alternate email accounts can be used for removing your data from aggregators, which is discussed in the next chapter, social media activity, booking hotel reservations, and nearly anything else you can think of that is noncritical to your financial or personal world.

One email provider you may not have considered previously but should is ProtonMail (https://protonmail.com). ProtonMail offers a secure email service with built-in end-to-end encryption that is not accessible by the company itself. Per the company website, they are incorporated in Switzerland with all of their servers also located in Switzerland. This is important, as the country has some of the strictest privacy regulations in the world.

Another service to consider is 33mail (https://www.33mail.com/), which is also a great privacy tool that offers unlimited, free disposable email addresses and acts as a forwarding service. Use 33mail to create an alias email address when your email contact is requested by online operators. All electronic communication sent by the operator will be sent through the alias and automatically forwarded to your account of choice (Gmail, ProtonMail, etc.).

As an example, if you were to sign up online with ABC Company, you could create an alias email specifically for ABC Company, such as abccompany@myalias.33mail.com. ABC Company would only see your 33mail email address and not your underlying actual email where the communication is being redirected to. When registering with 33mail, you would create a specific identifier that would be unique to you, such as "myalias," as used in the example above. The email will always end with .33mail.com, and you can alter the beginning part for each site and as many times as you want, such as "abccompany," as used in the example above. The only thing that will be constant will be your unique identifier and .33mail.com. You can instantly terminate the alias if the email communication becomes a nuisance or a breach occurs, all while leaving your actual Gmail, ProtonMail, or other email account private and secure.

> *Defensive tip:* Email is a very effective way for criminals to distribute viruses, ransomware, and other malware to home and corporate networks. Every second of the day, more than 2.8 million emails are sent out, with close to 70 percent of them being spam. It can be very difficult to spot the fakes when managing a large flow of email volume and even tougher when viewing the email over a smartphone with a smaller screen. All it takes is one click on a link or the opening of an attachment to infect your device. Before you click, test. Use the free scanning tool called VirusTotal (https://virustotal.com) to inspect either the link or attachment against more than seventy antivirus and URL blacklisting services. When viewing the email in question, hover over the link the sender is pointing you to, **right click**, copy hyperlink, and then paste into the URL tab within the VirusTotal website and scan. This will allow you to utilize the power of multiple cybersecurity tools all condensed in one site free of charge. If a hyperlink is malicious, this tool will likely let you know. You can either bookmark this site and visit it when testing or add it to your web browser as an extension.

CHAPTER 4

Data Aggregators: Know Who Has Your Information and How to Remove It

THE PERSONAL INFORMATION OF MOST adult consumers is collected, sold, and traded between hundreds of companies the majority of people have never heard of before. These organizations provide a goldmine of data for those who know where to find them. Such seekers of this prized information can include investigators, nosy neighbors, and cybercriminals, who access these sites in combination with other data-gathering techniques with the goal of building a detailed profile around a target's life and identity. However, when most people think about sensitive or private information, what typically comes to mind are medical records, bank account details, Social Security numbers, or payment card data. We displaced that myth in chapter 1. While this information is certainly highly confidential and must be properly secured, there is another category of data altogether that is often overlooked and very useful for criminals and investigators alike. This other category of "nonsensitive" information can be used for building a detailed profile on individuals, families, and businesses that will offer social engineering fuel to elevate the success rate of any attack. It will also give undesired third parties a deeper look into your life and social behavior.

Our full résumé and work history, where we went to school, years of graduation, lists of accomplishments, and other unique qualifications are shared on various social media and professional networking sites. Résumés are uploaded to job-seeker platforms that reveal additional data such as place of residence, email address, and other contact numbers. Website by website, social media platform by social media platform, and company by company, our digital footprints begin to expand and grow out of control. Here is where the privacy policy of that service we are entrusting our information to becomes all the more important. Who is the service selling our information to? Whom do they share it with for free? Who are their partners that have access? Who is scraping it without our knowledge or consent? These are all questions we need clear answers for, and it will typically come in the fine print. The problem is, no one likes reading through page after page of legalese.

A great deal of this information can be uncovered using various OSINT techniques when starting with a limited amount of public data concerning a target. An attacker will utilize various information sources, including the dark web, public forums such as Pastebin (a text-storing site for online information), social media accounts, and people search engines for verifying or rounding out a target's profile. You may not be familiar with some of these people search sites, but they definitely know you.

The benefit of becoming aware of these sites is that you can now start a personal assessment by conducting a search of your own name and family members within each company. I will provide links to the websites of several of these companies as well as opt-out links so you can remove your data. After a personal search is conducted, you might be surprised at how many details have been accumulated. Associated with your names will be your residence, past addresses, relatives, phone numbers, place of employment, annual income, your religious and political affiliations, neighbors, email addresses, and more.

You may wonder how these organizations get your information in the first place. One company explains via their website, "Our deep search robot continuously crawls the web and extracts names, locations, ages, images, facts, and other relevant information from general web documents, personal profiles, public records, phone directories, blogs, news articles, scientific publications, and many other types of pages; this data is then processed and indexed so it can be searched by anyone."

Another company that collects user cell phone and landline numbers states the following: "We use publicly available information, social media and user-contributed address books to provide names and photos for unknown or suspicious phone numbers and email addresses. This is stuff you would never find in a phone book—or .com directory websites based on phone books, white pages, or yellow pages!"

You may need to reread those statements. These organizations include people directories, data brokers, and marketers. As soon as one is shut down or your information is removed, two more will pop up in its place. Not only does their data collection feel intrusive but some also appear to have no regard for safeguarding the information they do collect. These data aggregators are reminders that we must think carefully about the content we choose to put online. This is especially critical for young users of social media and other technology services. The pictures you choose to post today or the website you provide your email address and phone number to could end up on one of these sites tomorrow. That can be a scary thought, especially when cyberbullying or -stalking is taken into consideration. All someone needs to do is visit a site, type in your name, and hit enter.

Notable breach: In 2018, a Florida marketing firm by the name of Exactis exposed a database of

340 million records, which was publicly accessible online and discovered by a security researcher. The information compromised in this incident was highly sensitive, as marking firms build detailed profiles that are used for targeted adverting by businesses. In this case, data included telephone numbers, home and email addresses, personal interests, and detailed information around households, including number of children, ages, and gender. This type of information is fuel for social engineering attacks and identity theft. The more an adversary knows about you, the greater the trust that can be built during a conversation over the phone (vishing or voice phishing) or through email exchange (phishing).

Take Action

Clean up your digital footprint by removing your data from these sites. It is important to know these organizations are not the originators of the information associated within your profile; they simply accumulate it from other sources. Much of this data originate from various government databases such as public voter registries, property tax records, and court records. Keep track of how and when you contact these organizations. Removing your information from these sites will reduce your digital footprint and make it harder for the casual snoop to find you. As a sidenote, I had to follow up with some sites multiple times before they finally took action. This is not an exhaustive list by any means, but it is a good start. Before you begin, create a few new email addresses for the specific purpose of removing your data.

Data Broker List and Removal Links:

Spokeo:

- Website: https://www.spokeo.com/

- Data removal/opt out: https://www.spokeo.com/optout

Neighbor Report:

- Website: https://neighbor.report/

- Data removal/opt out: https://neighbor.report/remove

Intelius:

- Website: https://www.intelius.com/

- Data removal/opt out: https://www.intelius.com/optout

BeenVerified:

- Website: https://www.beenverified.com/

- Data removal/opt out: https://www.beenverified.com/f/optout/search

PeopleFinders:

- Website: https://www.peoplefinders.com/

- Data removal/opt out: https://www.peoplefinders.com/about/help/top4

ThatsThem:

- Website: https://thatsthem.com/

- Data removal/opt out: https://thatsthem.com/optout

TruePeopleSearch:

- Website: https://www.truepeoplesearch.com/

- Data removal/opt out: https://www.truepeoplesearch.com/removal

MyLife:

- Website: https://www.mylife.com/

- Data Removal/opt out: Contact via email: privacy@mylife.com

- Privacy Policy: https://www.mylife.com/privacy-policy

Family Tree Now:

- Website: https://www.familytreenow.com/

- Data removal/opt out: https://www.familytreenow.com/optout

Nuwber:

- Website: https://nuwber.com/

- Data removal/opt out: https://nuwber.com/removal/link

Spy Dialer: This service provides the ability to extract the outgoing cellphone message you leave for missed calls.

- Website: https://www.spydialer.com/default.aspx

- Data removal/opt out: https://www.spydialer.com/optout.aspx

Whitepages:

- Website: https://www.whitepages.com/

- Data removal/opt out: http://www.whitepages.com/suppression_requests

TruthFinder:

- Website: https://www.truthfinder.com/

- Data removal/opt out: https://www.truthfinder.com/opt-out/

PeekYou:

- Website: https://www.peekyou.com/

- Data removal/opt out: https://www.peekyou.com/about/contact/optout/index.php

Instant Checkmate:

- Website: https://www.instantcheckmate.com/

- Data removal/opt out: https://www.instantcheckmate.com/opt-out/

MyRelatives:

- Website: https://www.myrelatives.com/

- Data removal/opt out: https://www.myrelatives.com/privacy

Instant People Finder:

- Website: https://www.instantpeoplefinder.com/

- Data removal/opt out contact via email: optout@instantpeoplefinder.com

- Privacy policy: https://www.instantpeoplefinder.com/privacy.html

Cyber Background Checks:

- Website: https://www.cyberbackgroundchecks.com/

- Data removal/opt out: https://www.cyberbackgroundchecks.com/removal

Acxiom:

- Website: https://www.acxiom.com/

- Data removal/opt out: https://isapps.acxiom.com/optout/optout.aspx

LexisNexis:

- Website: https://www.lexisnexis.com/en-us/gateway.page

- Data removal/opt out: https://optout.lexis-nexis.com

Cubib:

- Website: https://cubib.com/

- Data removal/opt out: https://cubib.com/opt-out.php

FastPeopleSearch:

- Website: https://www.fastpeoplesearch.com/

- Data removal/opt out: https://www.fastpeop-lesearch.com/removal

Private Eye:

- Website: https://www.privateeye.com/

- Data removal/opt out: https://www.people-finders.com/manage

People Wiz:

- Website: https://www.peoplewhiz.com

- Data removal/opt out: https://www.people-whiz.com/remove-my-info

PeopleByName:

- Website: http://www.peoplebyname.com/

- Data removal/opt out: www.peoplebyname.com/remove.php

CHAPTER 5

What Do Google and Facebook Know about You?

LET'S START THIS ASSESSMENT BY seeing just how much Google and Facebook know about you. We will conduct a self-assessment of your privacy settings and review what kind of sharing or data collection practices you grant each company. This is a practice that should be done with each and every service or app that you use. We will start with these two, as they are some of the largest and most far-reaching companies that we interact with, and the format will provide a blueprint to follow. It can be very easy to let these particular tech giants into all aspects of your life with how large they have become and how convenient the services make our daily routines.

The layout provided below will change with time, as companies consistently update their privacy policies, some more frequently than others, but this should at least get you familiar with the process and get you into the habit of checking.

Even if we take only a few of the Google-owned services such as Gmail, YouTube, Android, Chrome, Google Play, Waze, and Nest, the information collected can quickly add up. I have given presentations about data-collection practices and used Alphabet (parent of Google) as the example with an acquisition pace at one point that amounted to more than one company per week for two years. Many people may not remember this, but Google got into the mobile phone hardware game by purchasing Motorola Mobility for $12.5 billion in 2012.

So just how much does Google actually know about you? Find out by logging into your Google account to view what has been collected, and let's make any changes as needed to these practices. This portion of the book is designed to guide you while you are hands-on with each service. Also provided are the links needed for direct access. You will need to be logged in to your account to make the necessary changes.

Google:

- Your Location history: https://www.google.com/maps/timeline

Google states the benefits of collecting this data: Location History helps you get useful information—for example, automatic commute predictions, improved search results—by creating a private map of where you go with your logged-in devices. Location History is a Google Account-level setting that saves where you go *with every mobile device* where:

- You're signed into your Google Account,

- You have turned on Location History, and

- The device has Location Reporting turned on.

This practice is very intrusive and will accumulate your daily travel routine and locations of interest if you allow it. Note that the policy states they will collect all available information where you are signed in and will reach across devices (desk computer, tablet, and phone). Would you be comfortable with a stranger knowing the specific travel routines of you and your loved ones? Conduct a personal threat assessment, and ask what would happen if location information was leaked or obtained by bad actors.

> *Notable incident:* In 2017 users of a fitness-tracking app, Strava, had to grapple with this exact problem. The company released a global heatmap of their users' activity that broadcast and charted GPS location information on the fitness social network. A key issue here is that this map unintentionally gave away secret US military bases located throughout the world. Military personnel who were tracking and logging their

fitness routines in what was thought to be a harmless and competitive action were accidentally exposing military operations with locations that were previously unknown.

Turn Location History Off

You can turn off Location History for your account. On your Android phone or tablet:

- Open the **Settings** app

- Open the **Google** submenu

- Tap **Google Account**

- At the top, tap **Data & personalization**

- Under **Activity controls**, tap **Location History** and then **Manage setting**

- Change whether your account or your devices can report Location History to Google:

- Your account and all your devices: At the top, turn **Use Location History on or off**

If you're on a browser, go to the Activity controls section of your Google Account.

- Turn Location History off **(Pause)**

Now it is time to review your search and web history: https://myactivity.google.com/myactivity
Google explains if Web & App Activity is turned on, your searches and activity from *other Google* services (there are many, as highlighted above) *are saved to your Google Account*. This practice is far too intrusive and, if allowed, will quickly build a detailed profile of your interests and online behavior.

Turn Web & App Activity Off (Pause)

- On your computer, visit the Activity controls page. You may be asked to sign in to your Google Account

- Turn **Web & App Activity off**

Under the Activity controls page, make sure all of the following data collection and tracking options are toggled to "paused":

- Web & App Activity **(Paused)**

- Location History **(Paused)**

- Device Information **(Paused)**

- Voice & Audio Activity **(Paused)**

- YouTube Search History **(Paused)**

- YouTube Watch History **(Paused)**

To finish, go to "delete activity by" and:

- Delete by date: **today**

- Click **delete**

Facebook

Let's now turn our attention to Facebook. There are no shortage of privacy and security mishaps at this social media giant, which has more than two billion monthly active users. In an ideal privacy-minded world, the easy fix here would be to #deletefacebook. However, as a limited user myself, that may not be the simplest solution. The platform is clearly great for staying in touch with friends, exchanging photos with family members, and staying current on what your "friend" from high school who you have not talked to in over twenty years ate for dinner on Tuesday evening. There are certainly some pros with being on the platform, but there are also many cons. Although Mark Zuckerberg would disagree with my point of view here, I do not believe you are the owner of your data if you are on Facebook.

In 2012, Facebook entered into a consent decree with the Federal Trade Commission (FTC) for charges that it deceived users by failing to keep its privacy promises. A consent decree is defined as: "an agreement or settlement that resolves a dispute between two parties without admission of guilt or liability."

If we go right to the November 29th, 2011, press release, we can see the FTC complaint lists a number of instances in which Facebook allegedly made promises that it did not keep (but admitted no liability for doing so):

- In December 2009, Facebook changed its website so certain information that users may have designated as private—such as their Friends List—was made public. They didn't warn users that this change was coming or get their approval in advance.

- Facebook reassured users that third-party apps they installed would have access only to user information that they needed to operate. In fact, the apps could access nearly all of users' personal data—data the apps didn't need.

- Facebook told users they could restrict sharing of data to limited audiences—for example with "Friends Only." In fact, selecting "Friends Only" did not prevent their information from being shared with third-party applications their friends used.

- Facebook had a "Verified Apps" program and claimed it certified the security of participating apps. It didn't.

- Facebook promised users that it would not share their personal information with advertisers. It did.

- Facebook claimed that when users deactivated or deleted their accounts, their photos and videos would be inaccessible. But Facebook allowed access to the content, even after users had deactivated or deleted their accounts.

- Facebook claimed that it complied with the US-EU Safe Harbor Framework that governs data transfer between the United States and the European Union. It didn't.

Since this settlement, we have seen a security bug in 2013 that made private information such as an email address and phone number public to a user's connections. This impacted a mere six million people and was very minor compared to what was ahead. A year later Facebook conducted a mood experiment on more than five hundred thousand unknowing participants where news feeds were altered with positive or negative posts to measure how emotions spread across the platform. This practice is completely unethical, in my opinion. All during this time, Facebook was allowing app developers to consume troves of information on users' friends under the good intention of building apps that provided a better experience. More than likely, you were unaware that apps your friends were using had access to your personal information and were consuming every bit of information about you that they could. The Cambridge Analytica scandal blew the lid off of this practice when it was discovered a personality quiz app downloaded by roughly 270,000 participants allowed data to be collected on users' connections, which quickly added up to eighty-seven million Facebook users. It should be noted that Facebook did say they were sorry.

The FTC, which serves as the lead privacy watchdog in the United States and overseer of unfair and deceptive corporate practices against consumers, cannot levy fines against organizations on the first go-around when a consent decree is reached. These agreements will typically come with a twenty-year compliance period and require a change in behavior that must be adhered to by the company. They can, however, fine a company if that agreement is breached.

In July 2019 we witnessed history as the FTC issued a record-setting $5 billion civil penalty against Facebook for violations of the 2011 consent decree. By comparison, the largest penalty ever issued for a violation of a commission agreement was against Google in

2012 for placing advertising tracking cookies on consumers' computers, specifically in Apple Safari browsers, when it had agreed not to. That fine was $22.5 million. However, even with a fine the magnitude of Facebook's, which was more than double all of the previous worldwide privacy and security fines ever issued to organizations combined, many people were still not happy considering the 2018 annual reported revenue of $55.8 billion. This megafine could be considered a minor slap on the wrist; however, the greater benefit to users of the platform comes from the required change in behavior Facebook must now make, which includes a new privacy-compliance structure, designated compliance officers, and reporting processes, to name a few.

I mention this so you can reflect on whom your information is really being shared with. Most often, it may be many more people and companies than you realize. Also, something to consider is whether or not the company is following through on what they say they are doing within their privacy policy. With the recent fine against Facebook, the FTC said no, they weren't in this particular case.

The picture you post, the status update you make, location you check in to, and video you like is not only shared with your circle of connections. It is so much larger than that, and you need to be aware. You do not own your data. Some companies like to tell you that you own it, but their actions may show otherwise.

Now, realizing that you may be overexposed or sharing sensitive information with a broader group than anticipated, let's at least visit the privacy and security settings in the platform. While logged in to the desktop version of Facebook, navigate to the top right of the page, click the downward-facing triangle icon, **Settings,** and then **Privacy**

- Your Activity:

  - What can see your future posts: **Friends**

Review the two additional categories under Your Activity.

  - Review all of your posts and things you're tagged in

  - Limit the audience for posts you've shared with friends of friends or public.

Limit these categories based on your threat model/comfort level.

- How people find and contact you:

  - Who can send you friend requests: **Friends of Friends** is the most restrictive option

  - Who can see your friends list: **Only me**

- Who can look you up using the email address you provided: **Friends** is the most restrictive option

- Who can look you up using the phone number you provided: **Friends** is the most restrictive option

- Do you want search engines outside of Facebook to link to your profile: **No**

Timeline & tagging settings

Timeline:

- Who can post on your timeline: **Friends**

- Who can see what others post on your timeline: **Friends**

- Allow post sharing to stories: **Off**

- Hide comments containing certain words from your timeline: **Off**

Tagging:

- Who can see posts you're tagged in on your timeline: **Only me**

- When you're tagged in a post, who do you want to add to the audience of the post if they can't already see it: **Only me**

Review

- Review posts you're tagged in before the post appears on your timeline: **On**

- Review tags people add to your posts before the tags appear on Facebook: **On**

This section is very important for monitoring and managing what others are posting when it involves you. Here you can be aware and attempt to control content others post. This is particularly critical if you are a parent monitoring the pictures others are posting and tagging your children in.

Location

- This section should absolutely be set to **off**. Click the "view your location history" box to see what Facebook has collected on your whereabouts. You will need to reenter your password to access this data.

Face Recognition

- Do you want Facebook to be able to recognize you in photos and videos: **No**

This setting may be a futile effort, as your photos have likely been uploaded to the network, which does ultimately recognize you. Facebook has acquired multiple facial recognition software companies over the years, which apply machine learning algorithms that analyze not only photos once they are uploaded but from the smartphone camera itself in real time. You will see this in action when a box appears around a person's face within a photo. For this reason, I no longer upload any photos of my children to the platform. Since becoming much more privacy conscious, I have removed nearly all of the photos from my profile. I have specifically removed all photos of my children and family. Hardcore privacy enthusiasts would say that you should not have a Facebook account at all. You will need to assess your own needs and determine what is best for you.

Private Doesn't Mean Invisible

It is important to understand that even with the changes made to your privacy settings, information can still be gathered on you by means of various data-gathering techniques. This is in large part due to pictures and videos other people upload to the platform that may include you, groups you belong to (especially when the group is set to public), or items you choose to like, share, or comment on. It is important to be familiar not only for yourself but to educate your children as well. The youth are growing up in an age where everything they do and say is documented in some form online for the world to see and for someone who might be specifically looking. It can be a scary thought to know there are plenty of people who are actively looking. You can curb what will be available for others to find. Only post or share information with the mindset that it will be discoverable.

Virtual Scrapbook

Think for a moment about the digital trail and history that is cataloged by social media users today. Proud parents begin a child's life by documenting their date of birth with accompanying photos online for their network to see and like. These moments are life changing and joyful, ones that parents are excited to share—I know I was. From there, birthdays are celebrated and documented online. The first day of school is celebrated and documented online. School plays, musicals, sports, and other events are celebrated and documented online. Then, when a child is old enough, he or she will create an independent social media profile for use and further documentation. This profile will likely have the same last name of the parents, who have hundreds or thousands of pictures stored within their albums and/or the profile will be linked directly to the parents', indicating they are related. From here the youth may not even be aware of the basic privacy settings concerning their profile and how their posts are being shared outside of their network. They then begin creating a behavioral profile of themselves by liking, tagging, commenting, and uploading pictures and videos to the timeline and profile. The accumulation of data being generated on this young person has already become significant and is unlike anything his parents experienced growing up. All major events surrounding this young person's life have been recorded and cataloged, stretching all the way back to birth, and will be digitally linked between their personal profile and their parents'.

February 4th, 2004, is a day that changed information sharing and what it means to experience online privacy forever. This is the day that TheFacebook was launched by Mark Zuckerberg. The social networking site was previously active and operating under the name FaceMash as early as 2003 but quickly changed the name. I still remember my-then fiancée telling me about TheFacebook while I was hanging out with Tom on Myspace. For those who may not know, Tom was the Mark Zuckerberg of Myspace.

The information on social media platforms is searchable and can be used to the advantage of an adversary for building a false sense of trust with the child. An outsider that is able to learn their age, where they go to school, hobbies, places they have checked in, groups they belong to, and other points of interest can be used for building a very detailed profile. Creating trust is a significant factor in the success of a social engineering attack. The term *social engineering* in its simplest sense is a method used to manipulate or deceive a target. A perpetrator will try to achieve one of two things when carrying out a social engineering attack:

1. Have the target take action by clicking on a link or opening an attachment within an electronic communication. This can often result in the download of malware or a virus, which infects the computer or network. This is known as phishing when carried out through email or smishing when via text message. Smishing gets its name from SMS, which stands for short message service, and is how a text message is sent.

2. Give up sensitive information such as a username, password, Social Security number, or financial details. This can be carried out over

the phone, which is referred to as vishing (voice phishing) or through email or text.

Trust is what may allow one to accept a friend request from a person they don't know, open an email and click a harmful link or attachment, or give away sensitive information details such as a username and password. Social media platforms are an easy way for an adversary to find what appears to be commonalities or build a false sense of trust based upon all of the information that is so easily accessible. As parents and users of these platforms, it is critical that we do not hand it over on a silver platter ourselves. Also, as parents and educators of young users, it is critical we teach children the unintended consequences of oversharing and to be extremely selective on what data is specifically put out for the world to see. Information shared online is like toothpaste out of the tube. Once it is out there, there is no getting it back in the bottle.

The FBI reported in the Internet Crime report that social media platforms were used as the medium or tool to carry out more than $101 million of cybercrime losses in 2018. This does not include the additional $362 million of fraud for the confidence/romance scams that were also reported. Trust is at the heart of carrying out many of these crimes. The report highlighted that for all cybercrime captured in the 2018 report, victims under the age of twenty were targeted and scammed out of more than $12.5 million, while those over the age of sixty were the largest victim group and accounted for more than $649 million of fraud losses.

This is why it is so critical to understand the risks, reduce your privacy and security exposures, and become better educated on the dangers that exist online. Most people do not realize their information can be extracted by taking advantage of poor privacy settings by parents and children alike. Here are some key takeaways that will allow you to tighten up your digital profile and improve upon some key privacy practices:

1. Privacy settings on social media should be set at the strictest setting possible—especially as it relates to minors.

2. Minors should not use their accurate first or last name when creating social media profiles. Consider using an alias name. Do not include accurate details surrounding age, school, or location. This will greatly reduce the threat of identity theft when the data is compromised in a cybersecurity breach, reduce the concern when this data is shared by a company with business partners or advertisers, and will mask the true identity of the child, creating greater privacy.

3. Parents should reconsider all of the family details and milestones posted online that create a detailed profile of the child over time.

Refrain from linking your account to your child's profile.

4. Do not accept connections from people you do not personally know. Minors should especially be cautious when the potential connection shares many interests, hobbies, or appears to know a lot about the child.

5. Never give money to someone you only "know" via an online connection. Seniors are heavily targeted and scammed out of hundreds of millions of dollars each year, as detailed by the FBI.

6. Remember, trust is often at the center of building a false sense of security before a scam occurs. The information shared on social media platforms can be used for building a detailed behavioral profile, which can be used against you.

CHAPTER 6

Oh Grandmother, What Big Teeth You Have!

THIS MAY COME AS NO surprise to you, but sometimes people are not whom they claim to be. It can be hard enough to cut through fact versus fiction when meeting someone face to face, but the bar for discernment is significantly raised when navigating through the online world, where profiles and photos are fabricated and plagiarized with the intent to scam and manipulate unsuspecting victims.

Catfishing entered the spotlight in 2010 with a documentary that featured an online romance budding from a connection that started on Facebook. Ultimately, the star of the show, Nev Schulman, was deceived by a woman who pretended to be someone she was not. How she represented herself, her appearance, age, and life were all fabricated.

At its core, catfishing is pure dishonesty. This term is a social engineering technique given to a person who creates a fake identity with the goal of either bullying or deceiving someone else. Unfortunately, this scam can often end in heartbreak, financial loss, or fraud for the one being deceived. In the most recent internet crime report released by the FBI, confidence fraud/romance scams conned victims out of more than $362 million in 2018. This is the second-highest money maker for cybercriminals, and it involves no hacking of any kind. The only hacking being done is of another person's trust. The FBI defines confidence/romance fraud as:

- A perpetrator who deceives a victim into believing the perpetrator and the victim have a trust relationship, whether family, friendly or romantic. As a result of that belief, the victim is persuaded to send money, personal and financial information, or items of value to the perpetrator or to launder money on behalf of the perpetrator. Some variations of this scheme are romance/dating scams or the grandparent's scam.

I have seen and read about far too many cases of people looking for love only to be conned out of thousands or even hundreds of thousands of dollars because they led with their heart and trusted rather than taking a more skeptical approach by fully evaluating the situation objectively and without emotion. Does it make sense to wire transfer one thousand dollars to someone you have been speaking with online for only a couple of months but have never met before in person?

I would say probably not. Grandparents have sent thousands of dollars away to criminals who portrayed a stranded or jailed grandchild in need of money. This tactic of dishonesty takes many different forms. With all that said, can you be sure of who you are really connecting with and speaking to online when everything appears to check out?

Weeding out the bad apples is becoming harder and harder these days due to improvements in technology. Technology can both work for us and against us in our privacy and security fight. One method I often employ to investigate the validity of a profile picture is to conduct a reverse image lookup. Google is the most powerful tool for searching an image across the web. This method can help you identify a possible fraud or catfish attempting to connect with you or your children. With a typical catfish, a fraudster will find someone's social media account and assume their identity by taking their photos and creating an alternate account with a new name. A reverse image search of a profile picture or any additional pictures will scour the web for exact matches. Finding a match under a different profile and name will certainly raise a red flag. Google, Bing, and TinEye are a few tools you can use to spot a fraud. Navigate to the following sites to perform a reverse image search:

Google: images.google.com

- Click the camera icon

- Upload the image

Bing: bing.com/images

- Click the camera icon

- Upload the image

TinEye: tineye.com

- Click the arrow up icon

- Upload the photo

These are great tools to have in your arsenal and to be aware of to help spot scammers, but they are not bulletproof. A reverse image search may not spot a scammer who is using the photo of someone who has their social media profile set to private, and it certainly will not spot a unique, one-time image that has been generated by artificial intelligence.

Wait, artificial intelligence? What if the picture of the person used in the profile does not exist?

Here lies the greater concern, as real photos can also be created by computer programs in an effort to establish fake profiles, both for adults and children. A site by the name of thispersondoesnotexist.com will generate an endless supply of pictures with each page refresh. It is critical for not only adults to be aware but for our youth as well that people are not who they appear to be online. A ten-year-old talking with who appears to be another ten-year-old may very well turn out to be an adult. Profile pictures can be deceptive, and now they are easier than ever to fabricate. If we do not educate our children on the dangers of communicating and blindly trusting others online, the results can be devastating. The same can be true for a sixty-year-old woman looking for companionship. It is important to know both the defensive techniques of reverse image searching and the offensive measures of fake image creation to best protect your online well-being. The game has changed significantly since *Catfish* aired in 2010, and the methods used for fraudsters to evade detection have gotten better.

Play Defense

The offensive techniques described above are also a solid reason you would not want a child to use their actual picture as part of their profile or online identity. Including a minor's personal picture is overextending digitally and a real privacy risk where the consequences outweigh the benefits. Also, once content is shared online, consider it something that can never be retracted ever again. That picture of your child can be scraped by data brokers to build consumer profiles within their own database, copied and saved by any stranger who comes across it, used by a fraudster creating their own fake profile for scamming, or used without your consent for facial recognition software training.

Wait, what was that last part?

Yes, organizations developing facial recognition technology may use profile pictures scraped from various online sources to use as test subjects for improving the accuracy rates of their software without that individual's consent. Artificial intelligence and facial recognition technology require the analysis of hundreds of thousands of pictures in order to properly learn and differentiate facial features for improvements to be made. Part of a technology company's ability to improve could come from using your child as a test case. IBM published a report on the advanced study of fairness of facial recognition systems titled "Diversity in Faces" in January 2019. The goal was to "create AI systems that are more fair and accurate," as outlined in their research. The problem is that nearly a million of the photos used in the project were scraped from Flickr, an image-hosting site and video-hosting service. This was done without the affirmative consent of those individuals. This is just another reminder that once your photo or information becomes publicly accessible, you no longer have control of how it might be used and for what purposes.

Another reason to refrain from posting a minor's personal photo is that it may become archived in the Wayback Machine (https://archive.org/). Have you heard of it before? The Wayback Machine is a nonprofit operation that has built a digital and historical archive of the internet. Per the website, "We began in 1996 by archiving the Internet itself, a medium that was just beginning to grow in use. Like newspapers, the content published on the web was ephemeral—but unlike newspapers, no one was saving it. Today we have 20+ years of web history accessible through the Wayback Machine..."

As of this writing, the collection has 330 billion web pages stored just as they appeared on the day they were released. This means that if you want to see what the AOL webpage looked like in 2005, it can be pulled up and accessed just as it looked in 2005, including all photos and content featured at the time. You never know where a photo of your child could end up with the possibility of it being sealed in time on this public archiving platform.

CHAPTER 7

Your Online Movements Are Being Tracked. Cloak Your Activity

THE BROWSERS (GOOGLE CHROME, INTERNET Explorer, etc.) used to access the web allow trackers to identify us and trace our steps across the internet. In one study conducted by the Princeton Web Transparency and Accountability Project, one million websites were analyzed with the results highlighting that 76 percent of the sites visited had hidden Google trackers and 24 percent contained hidden Facebook trackers. The browsing habits and other data collected are then shared with advertisers and many other third parties who are interested in understanding where you spend time online.

To combat this, consider using a privacy-focused browser such as Firefox (https://www.mozilla.org/en-US/firefox/features/private-browsing/), made by Mozilla, a privacy-centric organization. The organization does collect information, so it is important to read the privacy policy in order to fully understand how they operate. Now, I know that reading an organization's privacy policy is typically not a fun-filled task, but I believe it's necessary if you want to know what information is at stake. A long, legalese-filled novel within the website accompanied by vague statements can be just as telling as a simple and transparent policy. If the policy is confusing and unclear, there may be a reason.

The Firefox browser can be hardened (increase your level of security and privacy) further by making custom adjustments in the *Privacy & Security* setting. Here are a few additional ways you can raise your personal privacy bar when using the Firefox web browser:

- Access the **Options** tab in the top right of the screen

- Click on **Privacy & Security** on the left side of the screen

- Scroll down to the bottom of the **Content Blocking** section

- Under "Send websites a 'Do Not Track' signal that you don't want to be tracked," click **Always**

Firefox goes on to provide some additional clarity around this option. As stated under *learn more*, "Most major websites track their visitors' behavior and then sell or provide that information to other companies. This information can be used to show ads, products or services specifically targeted to you. Firefox has a Do Not Track feature that lets you tell every website you visit, their advertisers, and content providers that you don't want your browsing behavior tracked. Honoring this setting is voluntary—individual websites are not required to respect it." Although websites do not have to abide by your request to be left alone, reputable organizations will honor the request. There is no downside to having this option selected.

- Under "Cookies and Site Data" check: **Delete cookies and site data when Firefox is closed**

In "learn more" Firefox explains, "Some websites have the ability to store information, such as files, in your local storage, and these files can only be removed manually by you. This helps the website run faster and prevents information from being lost if you lose your connection." Checking this box will keep your storage capacity from being cluttered and keep tracking pixels from being stored on your device by websites you seldom interact with.

- Under "Logins and Passwords," make sure both boxes for "Ask to save logins and passwords for websites" and "use a master password" are **unchecked**

It is poor security practice to have this sensitive information stored within your browser. If your computer were to become compromised, access to all of the sites where password and log in credentials were linked could be accessed and viewed by the attacker. Not having this information adds an additional layer of security to your personal cyber posture.

- Under the "Permissions" section, access the "settings" box on the right side of the screen each for "Location," "Camera," and "Microphone"

- **Check the box** at the bottom to "Block new requests for access"

- **Save changes**

This will prevent any site you visit from gaining access to these permissions unless you specifically grant them.

Make sure the following boxes are checked:

✓ Block websites from automatically playing sound

✓ Block pop-up windows

✓ Warn you when websites try to install add-ons

Having these boxes checked could prevent advertisements, malware, or viruses from being downloaded when visiting a website.

- Under "Firefox Data Collection and Use," **uncheck** "Allow Firefox to send technical and interaction data to Mozilla"

This will prevent additional computer usage information from being sent back to the Mozilla mother ship, adding a bit more privacy to your online experience.

- Locate the **Security** subsection

- Under "Deceptive Content and Dangerous Software Protection," **check the box** "Block dangerous and deceptive content"

Within the associated *learn more*, Firefox goes on to explain, "Firefox contains built-in Phishing and Malware Protection to help keep you safe online. These features will warn you when a page you visit has been reported as a Deceptive Site (sometimes called "phishing" pages), as a source of Unwanted Software or as an Attack Site designed to harm your computer (otherwise known as malware). This feature also warns you if you download files that are detected as malware."

These are good privacy and cybersecurity safeguards that can be added to your stock browser, especially when multiple people are using the same computer. These enhancements are readily available, and now you will be able to take full advantage of them to the benefit of your family's security posture.

Also consider adding uBlock Origin as an extension for greater protection.

- Within Firefox, go to **Options**

- On the bottom left, click **Extensions & Themes**

- Type "uBlock Origin" in the search bar at the top of the page

I tested this out myself by seeing just how many trackers and advertisements sit on the pages I visit online. As one example, I visited the Amazon website through my Firefox web browser with uBlock Origin and was notified that ninety pop ups/requests were being blocked from the main page alone. Visit the page for yourself and watch the number of blocked items slowly increase in the upper right-hand corner of your screen.

The privacy policy for uBlock Origin is one of my favorites. The privacy policy states the following:

- uBlock Origin does not collect any data of any kind.

- uBlock Origin has no home server.

- uBlock Origin doesn't embed any kind of analytic hooks in its code.

- uBlock Origin doesn't accept donations or any other form of financing.

- The only time uBlock Origin connects to a remote server is to update the filter lists and other related assets. If you disable auto-update in the "Filter lists" pane in the dashboard, uBlock Origin will not connect to any remote server, unless you click "Update now" and only if there are assets deemed "out of date."

As you can see, it is simple, transparent, and nonintrusive. If only more organizations followed this practice of being straightforward, brief, and privacy centric.

An additional practice to implement is the use of privacy search engine DuckDuckGo (https://duckduckgo.com/about) in place of others like Google or Bing. With DuckDuckGo, your search history won't be shared with third parties, and you can block hidden trackers embedded in the sites you visit. This is an organization that is committed to privacy, and they are interested in helping people de-Google their lives. They are financially motivated to do so.

Use a Virtual Private Network (VPN)

To further enhance your anonymity, consider using a virtual private network (VPN). A VPN encrypts all of your online traffic, masking it from your internet service provider and malicious prying eyes when connecting to public Wi-Fi. Think of it as a virtual tunnel providing privacy to the vehicle traveling through it. More importantly, a VPN will mask your true Internet Protocol (IP) address, which is the unique number linked to all of your online activity. Your IP address can expose your geolocation, where you work depending on the computer you are accessing, as well as the provider of your internet service. This is information that can all be used for tracking an individual and for spear phishing attempts. A spear phishing attack is a focused attempt at targeting a specific individual. If an adversary knows that you live in a certain location, such as Arlington Heights, IL, and have Comcast as an internet service provider, those pieces of information can be used against you in a targeted attack. It is all about building trust. The more information an attacker can accumulate and include within their communication to you, the greater the chance you may take the bait. The fewer details we reveal about ourselves, the harder it will be for an attacker to falsely establish trust, as they will have little to no available information to use in the deception.

There are several information-gathering tools, such as Canarytokens (canarytokens.org/generate) and GetNotify (getnotify.com), that can be embedded within emails and are used to capture a target's information without ever being detected. When a recipient opens an email with the invisible tracker planted from one of these services, details about the target's IP address, approximate location, internet service provider, and other information are sent back to the originator of the message. It is important to be aware that these services exist. The goal for operating safely online is to be aware of the tools and tricks adversaries use so that you can be better prepared and properly defend against them. A VPN will mask these actual details, making the information collected useless to the attacker.

OSINT Tip: Use Canarytokens or GetNotify to identify the IP address and general location of a person you have never met but connected with online. These tools will help you to further verify that your online connection is from where they tell you they are from location-wise. This can be an effective method for catching scammers who are looking to deceive you. I have seen many cases of people being taken advantage of by getting scammed out of thousands of dollars from their online connections who were not as they appeared to be. If the IP address is coming back to a location other than where they indicated they are from, this should raise a red flag. This tool can also be paired with the reverse image lookup methods mentioned in chapter 6 for a more complete investigation. Of course, this exercise will not be useful if the person is using a VPN.

Not all VPNs are created equal and should be researched before you make a selection. In this instance I prefer a paid service as opposed to free, as the VPN service provider will likely generate income by sharing your information or serving up additional advertisements. I personally use a provider by the name of Private Internet Access (PIA). I have no affiliation with this company and am a paying customer. I prefer this service for a number of factors that include cost, size of their server network, overall reputation, and the high regard privacy-minded professionals have for their brand. At the time of this writing, they also allow you to connect up to ten devices with your account, which will allow you to protect a multitude of computers and smartphones for your household.

Tip: How will you know if your VPN is actually working? Connect to the VPN and navigate to the site: https://browserleaks.com/. This will allow you to check the IP address being registered to your computer and will also provide a variety of additional security testing tools for managing your privacy.

Online Payments

For ultimate privacy, cash is king. In our digital society, paying with cash may not be convenient for most people or even possible in some situations, such as when making hotel or flight reservations. With this being the case, make it a priority to use a credit card in place of debit when choosing to purchase items online or at the gas pump. With a credit card transaction, funds are not taken directly out of your bank account, unlike a debit card purchase. Using a credit card will insulate your bank account in the event of fraud but offers nothing for your privacy. If you want to increase both your security and privacy, an additional step must be taken.

Service providers can help consumers take this next step with the ability to create secure virtual cards that mask true payment card details and identity. These masking services will give you a level of anonymity by allowing you to create burner (throwaway) cards that never reveal your true account details to the merchant.

As an example, the Starwood hotel data breach that was announced in late 2018 involved customer credit cards in addition to other personally identifiable information. The resulting threat for some is now payment card fraud for the affected individuals. The only way to remedy the situation would be to cancel the compromised cards and have the financial institutions reissue brand new cards. How many times has this happened to you? Rather than your having to go through this process over and over again, a compromised burner card would protect your actual account details, allowing you to simply dispose of the pseudo card and replace it with another. I have no affiliation with the following companies, but it is important to know they exist, especially if you find yourself using your debit card to make purchases online. Consider these two providers for achieving greater security and privacy:

- Free service (debit cards only) Privacy(dot)com company website: https://privacy.com/

- Paid service (credit cards) Blur company website: https://www.abine.com/

Brick and Mortar Stores Are Watching Your Every Step

When it comes to consumer data collection and analytics, online retailers have long had the advantage over physical stores. The gap is narrowing through the use of in-store consumer monitoring technology such as beacons. This technology is nothing new, but it is gaining greater adoption and is able to collect more about you whether you opt in or not. Bluetooth low energy (BLE) beacons use a low-frequency chip found in mobile phones and can communicate with beacon hardware devices within a store. The technology can even track you from LED light bulbs found within the stores. These information-gathering tools are being used in retail outlets, airports, and sports stadiums, to name a few examples. The tracking of your location, how long you stand in an aisle, or how many times you frequent a particular store may not seem like much to privacy un-enthusiasts, but when this data is paired with specific store apps and point of sale data tied to your credit card, the information collected and consumer profile assembled significantly changes.

> *Solution*: Turn your phone to airplane mode, dis-able Bluetooth, or try the unheard-of option, which is to enter a store without your phone. As a sidenote, the Bluetooth capability on your phone should always be turned off when it is not in use, as this can pose a security risk to your de-vice from hackers.

Your Phone Number Is the New Social Security Number

When you're thinking about the most sensitive types of information, your cell phone number probably does not initially come to mind. Likely, data such as a Social Security number, bank account and financial details, passwords, and medical records are what surface. Yes, this information is extremely sensitive, but what if I told you a phone number should be placed in this cat-egory as well? Hear me out. So much of what we do online is tied to our phone numbers these days. Some people may receive automated texts for a variety of service alerts: "Trash pickup is tomorrow," or while waiting at the restaurant, "your table is ready." A noble cause tied to a phone number can be to enable two-factor authentication (2FA) for an added layer of security when logging in to a website.

> *2FA explained*: Two-factor authentication is a combination of what you know and what you have. The "what you know" would be the password provided when logging in to a site. The "what you have" would be the phone in your possession to which a text would be sent with a numerical code. This number would then have to be entered into the site as well for that second layer of security to ensure it really is you.

The phone number is also used to communicate through phone calls and texts with family, friends, or even strangers when inquiring on a public posting for goods or services. We need our phone numbers when registering for social media accounts. Many families today have even done away with the landline, as the cell phone is typically no more than an arm's reach away and always accessible. But what is really in a cell number, and what harm could come from it falling into the wrong hands?

The DNA of Numbers

A phone number will reveal a lot of information about the owner, and there are many services that can be used to uncover that data. This becomes much more dangerous when the number belongs to a minor. Just as we discussed in chapter 4 on data aggregators and the importance of removing your listing, phone number-lookup services will provide detailed information that can tie back not only to the home address but other data such as the line type (mobile or landline), the carrier, location (zip), gender with some sites, as well as the full name the phone is registered under. This can all be revealed using only the phone number as your starting data point and nothing else.

Rare but Dangerous: SIM Swapping

This book has discussed various offensive- or OSINT-related tactics for the purpose of exposing how attacks could be carried out against an individual. Knowledge of these methods will allow for a stronger cyber defense and greater privacy awareness. Although the particular social engineering attack method I am about to cover is probably unlikely, it is still possible, as it has happened to others and will likely only increase in frequency from here on out. For that reason, it needs to be addressed.

This threat is a way to bypass a user's two-factor authentication by social engineering the cell service provider and is referred to as a SIM swapping attack.

Every smartphone has a SIM card, or subscriber identity module. This is a computer chip within the device and is what identifies you to the phone company. The SIM card effectively allows a user to place calls, send text messages, and connect to a mobile network.

In a string of recent Instagram account takeovers and cryptocurrency (digital money such as Bitcoin) heists, victims had their accounts compromised by attackers who canceled their phone service and in the process had their SIM card swapped to the criminal's own phone. This type of attack cost roughly forty victims $5,000,000 in digital currency from one attacker in particular, as reported by media outlets. By redirecting your incoming messages, criminals can easily complete the two-factor authentication checks that protect accounts, as the text message meant for you will now be sent to them. Even if you do not have two-factor authentication set up, a scammer can use your phone number to trick online service providers into resetting your passwords. The SIM-swapping investigative work requires a criminal to collect as much information on the target as possible, as they will need to pose as the target when calling the phone service provider. This is part of the reason why it is critical to remove your online presence from data aggregators (chapter 4) and to refrain from oversharing on social media platforms. Entering your phone number into a look-up service will tell the third party who your service provider is and what name the phone is under. Armed with this information and additional identifying factors such as your place of address, DOB, email contact, and other necessary data, which can be gathered from other sources, a call can be placed to your service provider (Verizon, Sprint, AT&T, etc.) in an effort to initiate the swap. Victims of this scam were alerted when their cell service suddenly went dead so it is important to be aware of this warning sign.

Tip: As an added layer of protection, set up a PIN number with your service provider. Having a PIN in place will not allow an attacker to so easily make changes to your account without also proving this additional information.

Number Lookup Service: Info tracer:

- Website: https://infotracer.com/ phone-lookup/

- Data removal/opt-out: https://infotracer.com/ optout/

Number Spoofing

Number spoofing allows a caller to mask or alter what appears on the caller ID for the person receiving the call. The ability to alter the caller ID offers both anonymity and increased privacy for a user but also presents an opportunity to deceive and harass if the motive is malicious. Many of the robocalls we receive each and every day are from numbers that have been spoofed to mimic a local call from our area. The practice of making a number appear local to the caller is referred to as neighbor spoofing. Number spoofing in general is not an illegal practice. Where this activity begins to cross the line is when the intent of the call is to defraud, cause harm, or wrongly obtain anything of value. Under the Truth in Caller ID Act, which is overseen by the Federal Communications Commission (FCC), perpetrators who illegally spoof calls can face penalties of up to $10,000 for each violation.

Scammers spoof numbers and change them frequently. You might even receive one of these calls appearing to come from your own number. Where this can become a serious problem is when cyberbullying or harassment is the focus. I participated in a news segment where a young high school teen was being harassed to the point of having to move, change schools, and change her phone number. It was undetermined who was behind the harassment, but the perpetrator(s) was spoofing this young person's number and making calls to her friends and other contacts pretending to be her. They were even arranging for strangers to show up at the victim's house and in one instance had someone from an escort service show up at the front door. The activity was unrelenting and occurred for years. This is an extreme case of cyber harassment and highlights why we need to be very selective with whom we share our phone numbers with, as it can have negative consequences if it ends up in the wrong hands.

The technology used to engage in number spoofing is readily accessible and at the fingertips of anyone who has access to the internet or downloads an app for their phone. Some of these services offer a number of features, such as allowing you to place a call that will go directly into voicemail without ringing the phone, alter your voice to appear as a man or woman, and can even add fake background noises that are not there.

For young people, the smartphone comes with a lot of responsibility. In order to limit the damage from number spoofing, SIM swapping, or having your true number exposed in data breaches, we can take advantage of this technology ourselves and for good use. Services such as MySudo or Google Voice will allow you to mask your actual number and set up an anonymous profile with a number of your choice that can be changed or discarded if it is involved in a company's cybersecurity incident. As of this writing, MySudo offers a one-year free plan that allows the use of one number with a limited number of monthly phone minutes and texts as well as unlimited use of an email account associated with the profile. Additional plans with a monthly cost will allow a user to have up to nine different numbers in use at one time. This will allow you to isolate your exposure, just as you should be doing with email addresses, as discussed in chapter 3.

These services assign what are called voice over internet protocol (VoIP) numbers. VoIP uses a standard internet connection to make phone calls. These are virtual numbers assigned to a person but not an actual phone line. You can segment your risk by using a specific phone number for friends, one for family, and others for shopping or any other place requesting a contact number. Anyone who researches these numbers through a lookup service will not find your service provider details. This offers an additional barrier for anyone trying to initiate a SIM swap attack, as it protects your true phone number. Also, in the event of harassment, such as spoofing friends or family, the perpetrator would have to obtain access to all of the different numbers you use if you segment your activity in this manner. Trying to spoof your number with one friend may work, but once they move on to others, the bully's luck would run out, as the number your additional contacts have for you would be different. If harassment occurs, a user can simply discard that specific number and set up a new one in its place. There will be no need to cut off service or change your actual phone number with the phone carrier.

Here are the links to MySudo and Google Voice. Utilize one or both of these services for achieving greater privacy and security by protecting your actual phone number and telecom details:

- MySudo: https://mysudo.com/

- Google Voice: https://google.com/voice

Do you have a minor with a phone? Consider this tip: To help with blocking robocalls or scam calls to the phone of your child, implement the most privacy-focused option already available within the phone itself: Do Not Disturb. The Do Not Disturb function can be activated to only allow calls from numbers programed within the contact list to come through. This will force any other numbers not already programmed into the device's voicemail. Preprogram any key contact such as family, friends, or the child's school to allow these calls to ring and be answered.

While there are apps that can be downloaded that work to block unwanted calls, an article from media outlet Tech Crunch revealed that users who downloaded various apps had their phone numbers shared with analytics firms and information such as device type and software version to other companies without the users' explicit consent. Any time an app is downloaded or software is installed, there is always a risk of users' information being shared with third parties. In fact, this is most often the case. It is critical to read the privacy policy of these services, but they may not always be clear about their data-sharing practices. The Do Not Disturb function is noninvasive and is already available on the phone's current features. Take the following steps to set up this option for the iPhone or Android devices:

iPhone:

- Settings

- Do Not Disturb

- Toggle on Do Not Disturb

- Allow Calls from: All Contacts

As an emergency feature, you can activate a setting called Repeated Calls. This setting will allow a call to come through from a number that is not programmed if two calls from the same number are made within a span of three minutes.

Android:

- Swipe down from the top of the screen to open the notifications

- Select Do Not Disturb

- Tap Do Not Disturb using your predefined settings. If you want to make changes to your settings, hold on the Do Not Disturb icon to go into the Settings menu. From the Settings menu, three sections will be available: Behavior, Exceptions, and Schedule.

- Exceptions will allow you to white list specific contacts

- Under Calls, you can configure specific contacts you want to come through while Do Not Disturb is turned on. There is an option to make it starred contacts only. You can customize starred contacts in the Contacts app of your phone

There is also a feature that allows repeat callers to get through in the event of an emergency if you get two calls from the same number within a fifteen-minute time period.

Who Is Listening?

Have you ever used the talk-to-text feature within the Facebook messenger app, participated in a Skype call, used Cortana or Siri to ask a question, or have an Amazon or Google digital assistant in your home? If the answer is yes, then they all have one thing in common: someone was listing to you. Well, maybe not you specifically, but all of these major technology brands were called into question over their less-than-transparent disclosure of using human contractors to eavesdrop on people's voice recordings. Actual people, not only artificial intelligence software, were being hired to review what was in many cases intimate conversations all in the name of improving upon their products and services. Several media outlets previously reported on this practice, which prompted the tech companies to publicly respond. For example, Microsoft amended their privacy policy by providing clarity and attention to the human element of voice data inspection. This change was made after media outlet Motherboard first reported about how Skype users who accessed the app's translation service and audio recordings captured by the Cortana voice assistant were being reviewed by actual people.

A snippet of the US Microsoft privacy policy is now as follows and appears under the section "How we use personal data":

> Our processing of personal data for these purposes includes both automated and manual (human) methods of processing. Our automated methods often are related to and supported by our manual methods. For example, our automated methods include artificial intelligence (AI), which we think of as a set of technologies that enable computers to perceive, learn, reason, and assist in decision-making to solve problems in ways that are similar to what people do. To build, train, and improve the accuracy of our automated methods of processing (including AI), we manually review some of the predictions and inferences

produced by the automated methods against the underlying data from which the predictions and inferences were made. For example, we manually review short snippets of a small sampling of voice data we have taken steps to de-identify to improve our speech services, such as recognition and translation.

In the case of Facebook, Bloomberg reported a program was in place where workers would listen to users' personal conversations on its Messenger app. This practice was being done to transcribe Messenger audio chats.

The moral of the story is that you never know who might be listening when accessing talk-to-text features or using your voice to initiate commands with technology products. Biometric data (unique physical characteristics) such as your voice will become more common in the use of authentication as we move into the future. If a compromise of this information occurs where an organization entrusted with it was not able to protect it, there is no canceling and reissuing products, as is the case with credit cards. Your voice is your voice. In addition, I ask you to reflect for a moment on how comfortable you feel knowing that someone could be listening to your private chats or the conversations taking place within the privacy of your home. This is not a matter of having nothing to hide, as most of us have nothing to hide. This issue is a right to privacy. Can you truly be yourself if you know someone is always watching or listening? What could be the next device or company that decides it needs to monitor your conversations in the name of quality improvements? If you must use these services, at the very minimum, be aware of the risks and how a company uses your information.

CHAPTER 8

Where There's a Wi-Fi, There's a Way

DO YOU REMEMBER THE DAY your internet service provider came into your household and set up your wireless router, giving you access to the internet? What you did during those moments of installation is much more important to your home security than you may have realized.

First, let's cover some of the basics. A wireless router allows you to connect your computer and other devices to the internet. A SSID (Service Set Identifier), more commonly known as a Wi-Fi network name or hotspot, is then created and broadcast, allowing your devices to connect and gain access to an online network. The setup and configuration of your router and Wi-Fi access can create significant security and privacy vulnerabilities for your household if not done properly. I am going to cover the offensive side discovering Wi-Fi vulnerabilities so you can look through the eyes of a potential hacker and use it to strengthen your home security.

Wardriving

The OSINT technique known as wardriving is the practice of actively scanning and collecting Wi-Fi network names and all associated information by a person in a car using a laptop or smartphone. If someone has the software on their phone and they happen to drive by your home, all of your information can be swept up, creating a security and privacy danger to you and your family. I encourage you to look at one such service for yourself at *wigle.net*. By using this service, you can review your state, city, block, or individual residence to see what Wi-Fi network data has been collected and shared with the site. If you want to search only by SSID names, you can do that as well (FBI Stakeout Van, Nachowifi, etc.).

Here is how it works: individuals download the WiGLE app, which will collect wireless network information as they drive around businesses, residential streets, and everywhere in between. They can then choose to upload that information to the site, which will be shared with other WiGLE users as well as the general public who know the site exists.

Now that you are aware, this information can be used to your security awareness advantage. The reason you need to know the practice of wardriving exists is that it collects the following important information:

- Geographic location

- Wi-Fi network name

- When the information was first captured and most recently captured

- Type of security/encryption used with your wireless network

Let's discuss why each of these four points matters to your home security. First is the geographic location of your home. This will pinpoint your specific residence or place of business, allowing not only the individual who collected your information to see it but anyone who accesses the WiGLE map if that data was uploaded. The home or business address is not specifically collected; however, the latitude and longitude coordinates are included with the ability to view a map of the location, which provides all the details needed to pinpoint an address. This information will lead someone right to your front door and for obvious reasons would be an invasion of your privacy and security.

The next critical data point collected is the Wi-Fi network name (SSID). Many people either leave this as the brand of the router (Netgear, Linksys, D-Link, etc.) or use their own first and/or last names. Using the brand of the router is a big mistake, as you may be giving away certain security vulnerabilities that have been discovered but not patched by the company. Also, many routers are shipped with default usernames and passwords such as admin/admin or admin/password. These default lists are accessible to anyone who conducts an online search of "router default username and password." If someone knows the specific router you have and you did not change the username and password when the initial setup was done, your security is in serious jeopardy. If an adversary gains access to your router, the following could occur:

- Your internet traffic could be redirected to malicious sites. For example, when doing online banking, you could be diverted to a phishing site that looks exactly like the log in page of your actual financial institution.

- Malware planted by the intruder could be installed on any of your connected devices.

- All other devices connected to the router could be accessed and compromised.

- All other connected devices could be used as part of a larger botnet to attack (DDoS) third parties.

For the reasons mentioned above, it is absolutely critical that the security of your router be a priority. Next on the WiGLE list is the date information was first captured as well as most recently captured. This will give you an idea of how frequently your location is being scanned. You need to be mindful of when your router was initially set up and of the security settings that were put in place at the time. This will take us to the last point, and that is the security/encryption used with your router.

Wireless Encryption

Wired Equivalent Privacy (WEP) was the Wi-Fi security standard introduced in 1999 and has been the most widely adopted security protocol employed world-wide. The problem today is that many people are still using this method, which is now outdated, vulnerable to hacking, and multiple versions behind what is currently available. If the security associated with your Wi-Fi name is listed as WEP, you can be seen as an easy target for hacking. A novice hacker could search online for "how to hack WEP encryption," and the results would provide countless step-by-step instructions for achieving this.

The next generation of security, released in 2003, was called Wi-Fi Protected Access (WPA), followed by Wi-Fi Protected Access II (WPA2) a few years later. Stronger encryption and data protection methods were introduced with these later versions, removing the flaws found in WEP.

Now that you understand all of this information, there are some steps that need to be taken to enhance your security and increase your privacy. Every router is different and will require you review the manual (if you still have it somewhere) or locate the digital version online by searching for the manufacturer's support page. Here are some basics to get you started:

1. Identify the router IP address to access the router's settings. If you are operating on a Windows computer, do the following:

   - For Windows 10, type "cmd" in the Cortana search field in the bottom left side of the screen. Hit enter.

   - Type "ipconfig" and hit enter.

   - Under the heading "Ethernet adapter" will be a column for Default Gateway. To the right of that will be your router's IP address. *Remember that number.* Close the window.

   - Enter the router's IP address into the address field of your web browser. Hit enter.

   - Here, you will need to enter your username and password. If this is the default that came with the router, it should be changed to a unique set immediately.

2. Change your SSID (wireless network name). Do not choose a name that identifies your family or identity. Remember, this name is captured through the process of wardriving, and you do not want an identifiable name associated with your residence.

3. Consider hiding your network name. This will prevent the SSID from being broadcast to most wireless devices looking for a connection. This is not bulletproof, however, as there are devices that can still capture hidden network names. This will offer privacy from the typical nosy neighbor or novice hacker.

4. Enable WPA2 encryption.

5. Establish a guest Wi-Fi network. This will create segmentation between important connections—such as your home computer, which might be used to access financial accounts and other sensitive information—from IoT devices like a printer, coffee maker, or a visitor to your home.

CHAPTER 9

In the Name of Privacy, Disinformation Is Acceptable Information

AS DISCUSSED IN PREVIOUS CHAPTERS, where we live, work, our phone numbers, email address, family members, wireless network name, employment history, and other contact information is scraped, scanned, breached, sold, and traded among countless organizations and public entities. If you are not muddying up the waters on the accuracy of this data, then let this be your invitation to start getting dirty. In this book we have covered several measures we can take defensively to remain anonymous online. This is now the offensive side of privacy, creating misinformation.

Giving social media platforms and other organizations data to associate with your name is in stark contrast to the core strategy of this book, which has been all about data minimization and removal. The tactic of providing incorrect information associated with your name will actually provide additional cover and offer greater privacy, as it will make it considerably harder for anyone trying to put an accurate profile together regarding your location, interests, contact information, and other identifying characteristics. Data breaches at organizations holding your misinformation will not elevate your future risk of identity theft, which is also an added benefit.

There are a number of things you can do to deliberately associate disinformation with your name or home address. Consider signing up for a news subscription using an alias name but leaving your home address as accurate data. You can be assured this information will be sold or shared with third-party companies, which will pollute the actual data of who lives at the residence (see list of data aggregators in chapter 4). This tactic will associate multiple names with your home address once it is picked up by data brokers and aggregators, making it difficult to determine who actually resides at the location on file. We already discussed ways to opt out and remove your data from these sites. The only data these aggregators need to have on you is inaccurate data. Creating false information will over time repopulate and pollute the information that is publicly associated with your identity.

This same strategy can be done with telephone numbers and home addresses. There are no shortages of online or in-store contests that ask for names, email addresses, and other contact information from participating individuals. Provide a mix of true and pseudo details when completing these entry forms. A real name combined with a fake phone or home address will do the trick.

As a sidenote, never provide the home residence of another person as misinformation. This tactic would be wrong and unfair to the unsuspecting person whose home address you are using. When evaluating a false address to use with your name, consider creating an address that is nonexistent and does not impact any true residence. Remember, this tactic is not to be used for the purposes of receiving any real mail or content of any consequence. These contests are data-sharing nightmares and can be used to your full advantage when creating misinformation. Oak Valley Street, Sunset Dr., or W. Golf Lane are pretty generic. Add a number, zip, and state, and make sure you double check it does not exist. Running a quick search in Google Maps should get the job done.

Regarding telephones, there are numbers you can provide that will always be busy when dialed. The following numbers can be provided when offering misinformation to associate with your name. Providing this misinformation is different than using your VoIP (MySudo or Google Voice) telephone number, which is a tactic to protect your privacy but still serves as a functional number for actual use. Remember, this strategy is being done to muddy the waters between real and inaccurate data that will be accessible by third parties who are looking or used by companies and advertisers from all of the data-sharing practices that take place. If you use your VoIP number, it will become associated with your name, which defeats the purpose of this tactic. Consider these numbers for use:

Busy Signal Numbers:

- Los Angeles Area Code: 909-661-0001 through 909-661-0090

Be sure to always test the number before you decide to associate it with your name. Again, never provide the actual phone number of another person or business when using this strategy.

Consider altering some personal information on your social media accounts to add further inaccuracies. Provide a fictitious high school, year of graduation, date of birth, or hometown. Provide an inaccurate place of employment or work history. You are doing nothing wrong in providing this misinformation, as this is your own personal bio. Understand that it is being scraped constantly by companies without your consent or knowledge—at least it has been until now. If they are going to insist on scraping your data, then go ahead and give them something to take, but allow it on your own terms. Much of this data is shared with and collected by data brokers and will populate inaccurate information over time. This will also throw anyone off the mark who might be trying to obtain details on you, which can provide fuel for social engineering attacks. As an example, if you were to receive an email out of the blue from someone who claimed to go to your fictitious high school or knew you from an incorrect hometown or place of employment, you will be better prepared to defend against such targeted threats.

As it relates to social media platforms specifically, far too much information is regularly given away. This is an area where strong privacy practices can be developed at a young age and carried out through adulthood. Educate your children on the importance of reserving what you choose to share and whom it is being shared with. You never know who is looking. Here is an instance where sharing inaccurate information can be to your benefit. Many security-related questions surrounding passwords can be found in the treasure trove of data shared through social media sites. Where you grew up, hometown, children, pets, and anniversaries are regularly used for passwords and answers to security questions when people forget their passwords. Don't make the job of a hacker easy. First and foremost, don't share all of this information, especially if you are using it in relation to your passwords. Second, provide inaccurate data.

When registering with noncritical websites, do not provide your actual name, date of birth, or primary email address. This is especially true of connected devices and interactive toys for children, which we discussed in chapter 2. When this information is eventually compromised or mishandled by the organization itself, it will have much less of an impact on your actual identity. I do not believe any accurate information on children should ever be shared with companies that are not medical or government related. There is no need for apps on phones, connected toys, or items of personal interest to ever require identifiable details on minors.

As an example, one of my sons was invited to a birthday party where all of the children needed to pre-register for a session of laser tag. The facility asked for the child's name, age, and required an email address. During the registration process, I provided an alias name and used my 33mail forwarding account to mask my actual email address. I also created an alias "username" for my son that was displayed on the televisions within the facility for tracking his gaming stats while playing. If the database is ever compromised, I have no concerns, as identifiable information was never provided. (Side note: never provide false information to government, law enforcement, financial, or health-care providers.)

The more we can use this tactic with organizations that do not require our true information, the better off we will be when a cybersecurity incident occurs. Data breaches will continue to happen, so we must take the necessary steps to protect our information if companies won't.

Our youth must limit what true details are being provided for the world to see on these social media platforms. There is nothing wrong with taking part online through a variety of networks, but it must be done so responsibly. Minors who want to participate in the online social networking world will be able to connect with their real friends, as true friends can be told where to find their profile. It is important to remember that once connections are made with friends, you cannot control what others post, and if it involves your child, it could be putting their privacy at risk. Children must be educated of the online dangers that exist and understand how to limit their overall exposure where it makes sense.

Knowing that data brokers, information aggregators, and a host of other companies work every second of the day to scrape this information should be enough of a warning to share sparingly or at least inaccurately.

CHAPTER 10

The Credit Freeze

BEFORE THE EQUIFAX DATA BREACH of 2017, freezing your credit was a very good idea and effective risk-mitigation tool for lowering your chances of identity theft. Now, nearly two years after the Equifax breach ripped through the headlines and impacted nearly every adult in the United States, it is still a very good idea. So what has changed? As a result of the credit reporting agency's massive security failure that involved nearly 150 million individuals—data that included people's names, Social Security numbers, birth dates, home addresses, and, for some, driver's license information—congress passed into law new protections for consumers surrounding identity theft risk management.

Effective September 21, 2018, the Economic Growth, Regulatory Relief, and Consumer Protection Act went live, giving consumers the ability to freeze and unfreeze their credit files absolutely free of charge. Prior to the law passing, it would have cost an individual $5–$10, depending on your state, per credit-reporting agency, to freeze your credit report. As there are three national credit reporting bureaus, this could cost up to $30 per person to initiate this protection.

In my opinion, freezing your credit is a must if you are serious about protecting your identity and reducing the likelihood of fraud occurring. The cost to take advantage of this risk reduction tool is no longer a barrier. When a freeze is implemented, potential credit lenders will not be able to access your credit file/history to determine whether or not a line of credit should be extended in your name. The lender will be unable to determine your creditworthiness because access to your history will be prevented. This part is critical for reducing the risk of another person opening a new line of credit in your name. Here is the formal definition of security freeze under the new law:

> The term "security freeze" means a restriction that prohibits a consumer reporting agency from disclosing the contents of a consumer report that is the subject of such security freeze or, in the case of a protected consumer for whom the consumer reporting agency does not have a file, a record that is subject to such security freeze to any person requesting the consumer report for the purpose of opening a new account involving the extension of credit.

The request to freeze your file can be done either online or over the phone with each of the national credit reporting agencies for consumers age sixteen and older. Under this consumer protection law, when requesting the freeze either online or by phone, the bureau will have one business day to place the freeze. If the request is made by mail, the bureau will have three business days. Consumers will then receive written confirmation no later than five business days after the freeze is placed, which will include details of the process to remove/lift this freeze when needed. Save this information in a safe place, and do not lose it! There is a tight timeline that must be adhered to by the bureaus, which is good for all of us, as a sense of urgency is being adopted.

Many times I have been asked the question, "What if I need to take out a loan or have a credit check done and my report is frozen?" This process is easy and has actually improved for the consumer since the new law has passed. In this case ask the lender which bureau they plan to contact.

Going back to the confirmation paperwork each bureau sends that was mentioned above, you will find a PIN number that is unique to your file and must be provided for unfreezing and refreezing your credit file. Use this PIN to unfreeze your credit with the appropriate bureau. If the removal request is made over the phone or online, they will have one hour to lift the freeze. If the request is made via mail, three business days will be given. This allows anyone the ability to move quickly when needed. The security freeze should not be a hindrance; it is a useful tool for reducing your identity theft risk. It is important to know what is available to you as a consumer and to take advantage of those protections.

In order to obtain your free freeze, you must contact each of the agencies individually by website, phone, or mail. Below are the current contact numbers and website URLs to start the process for anyone sixteen years of age and older.

- Experian: 888-397-3742

- Website: https://www.experian.com/freeze/center.html

- TransUnion: 888-909-8872

- Website: https://www.transunion.com/credit-freeze

- Equifax's automated security freeze system: 800-349-9960

- Website: https://www.equifax.com/personal/credit-report-services/

Now, the process for minors (those defined as under the age of sixteen) or the category known as "protected consumers" is a little bit different and more of a cumbersome process than described above. Under the law, protected consumers include minors and incapacitated persons or a protected person for whom a guardian or conservator has been appointed. These are vulnerable members of society and must be protected. Prior to the law, it was not possible to freeze the credit report of a minor unless one was already created. The only way a credit file would be created was if someone committed identity theft using their name. Minors make good targets, as the fraud can go undetected for years. Typically, it would not be until the child becomes a young adult and applies for that first credit card or might be heading off to college when it is finally discovered that their credit history has been ruined before it could be established legitimately.

As parents or guardians, we no longer have to use the credit freeze as a reactive response to identity theft but now have the ability to utilize it as a proactive tool prior to any damage occurring in the first place. This process must be handled by mail and requires the parent or guardian to collect and submit very sensitive details proving your guardianship as well as information on the protected consumer. No online or phone options exist currently. The formal instructions with each bureau are provided below.

Placing a Security Freeze for Protected Consumers

- Experian: https://www.experian.com/freeze/form-minor-freeze.html

- TransUnion: https://www.tran-sunion.com/credit-disputes/child-identity-theft-inquiry-form

- Equifax: https://assets.equifax.com/assets/personal/Minor_Freeze_Request_Form.pdf

There are many misconceptions when it comes to freezing your credit. First, doing so does not lower your credit score. In fact, it may help to maintain or increase your score, as soft pulls against your file will be rejected. Inquiries on your credit file can slowly chip away at your overall score. A freeze will prevent that from occurring. Second, a freeze does not lock out or prevent fraud from occurring on any current lines of credit you have open. Those relationships will continue to exist, and a bad actor could commit fraud with any open credit you maintain.

Summary and Additional Resources

MY GOAL FOR WRITING THIS book was to help prepare the family by making smarter choices online. This topic can be very overwhelming, but as parents, we cannot shy away from it. We are raising children in a world where very little remains private and where the physical world continues to become more connected with the virtual one. We must do our best to protect our children and teach them how to be responsible technology users or the digital road ahead will be a tough one. Likely much tougher than what we experienced growing up, as the connectivity and availability of data was only a fraction of what it is today. We had privacy. Children today do not. Our actions have to be intentional if achieving greater privacy is the goal. Gaining a greater level of anonymity and security online will not happen by accident. My hope is that this book will provide the needed blueprint to help you do that successfully.

This process will be one that never ends, as we must continue to adapt our methods while technology continues to change. Arming our children with the proper knowledge will help develop lifelong good habits that will be to their advantage in the long run. Some of these practices are so simple yet very powerful in offering a needed layer of protection in the event a data breach occurs and our information is exposed. Half the battle is to understand your threats and reduce your exposure where possible. Apply the methods that were discussed over time, as they do not all need to be done overnight. This is a process. As a matter of fact, you may find that some of these tactics will not be a part of your routine at all if they address issues you are not particularly concerned with, such as using the voice-to-text capabilities within an app. I want you to be aware of the risks and make the conscious decision to either accept that risk or reduce it. Being informed is critical.

In closing, I want to provide some additional resources to be used at your disposal and available on demand when needed. I have participated in numerous televised news and radio segments surrounding corporate data breaches, identity theft, and privacy-specific topics. Some of these clips include the advice and methods I have shared throughout the course of this book as well as additional insights on security. For the visual learner, these news segments may help add greater clarity to what has been covered within previous chapters or could be shared with friends and family for guidance on how to live and interact more securely online. While these clips have been tied to previous breaking news events that have come and gone, the underlying advice is still as relevant as ever. I hope you will find these resources beneficial.

Roseville mom: Cyberbullying of daughter has led to phone spoofing:

- http://www.fox2detroit.com/news/local-news/roseville-mom-cyber-bullying-of-daughter-has-led-to-phone-spoofing-harassment

Cyber expert warns of Face App, bank account threats:

- http://www.fox2detroit.com/news/local-news/cyber-expert-warns-of-face-app-bank-account-threats

Michigan ranks eight in internet fraud loss. Here's how to protect from online scammers:

- http://www.fox2detroit.com/news/local-news/michigan-ranks-8-in-internet-fraud-loss-here-s-how-to-protect-from-online-scammers

How can you avoid getting information stolen online? Confuse the culprits:

- http://www.fox2detroit.com/news/local-news/how-can-you-avoid-getting-information-stolen-online-confuse-the-culprits

Talking cybersecurity for smart homes—what you should know:

- http://www.fox2detroit.com/news/local-news/talking-cyber-security-for-smart-homes-what-you-should-know

Cybersecurity expert: High-tech toys could put children at risk:

- http://www.fox2detroit.com/news/local-news/cyber-security-expert-high-tech-toys-could-put-children-at-risk

How to spot a credit card skimmer with a special trick:

- http://www.fox2detroit.com/news/local-news/how-to-spot-a-credit-card-skimmer-with-a-special-trick

How to secure your data online with local expert David Derigiotis:

- https://www.fox2detroit.com/news/351789250-video

Millennials and Money | Easy Money with Murray Feldman:

- https://www.youtube.com/watch?v=gyp26YBiNtw&feature=youtu.be

References

- Bloomberg Fortnite: https://www.bloomberg.com/news/articles/2018-11-26/fortnite-now-has-200-million-players-up-60-from-the-last-count

- Busy numbers: Hiding from The Internet. Eliminating Personal Online Information. Fourth Edition. Author, Michael Bazzell

- Economic Growth, Regulatory Relief, and Consumer Protection Act: https://www.congress.gov/bill/115th-congress/senate-bill/2155

- Wardriving: https://en.wikipedia.org/wiki/Wardriving

- WiGLE: https://www.wigle.net/

- TineEye: https://tineye.com/

- FBI IC3 Report: https://www.ic3.gov/media/annualreports.aspx

- Internet live stats: https://internetlivestats.com

- FTC: https://www.ftc.gov/news-events/blogs/business-blog/2019/07/ftcs-5-billion-facebook-settlement-record-breaking-history

- CNBC Facial Recognition: https://www.cnbc.com/2019/03/12/millions-of-photos-scraped-without-consent-for-facial-recognition.html

- IBM Report: https://www.ibm.com/blogs/research/2019/01/diversity-in-faces/

- California Civil Code: https://codes.findlaw.com/ca/civil-code/civ-sect-1798-80.html

- Nest: https://www.washingtonpost.com/technology/2018/12/20/nest-cam-baby-monitor-hacked-kidnap-threat-came-device-parents-say/

- State Farm Credential Stuffing: https://www.govinfosecurity.com/state-farm-investigates-credential-stuffing-attack-a-12893

- Data Breach Notification Laws: https://www.foley.com/en/insights/publications/2019/01/state-data-breach-notification-laws

- uBlock Origin privacy policy: https://github.com/gorhill/uBlock/wiki/Privacy-policy

- TechCrunch: https://techcrunch.com/2019/08/09/many-robocall-blocking-apps-send-your-private-data-without-permission/

- Microsoft Privacy Policy: https://privacy.microsoft.com/en-US/privacystatement

- Revealed: Microsoft Contractors Are Listening to Some Skype Calls: https://www.vice.com/en_us/article/xwegbq/microsoft-contractors-listen-to-skype-calls

- Bloomberg: https://www.bloomberg.com/news/articles/2019-08-13/facebook-paid-hundreds-of-contractors-to-transcribe-users-audio

- Video Social Networking App Musical.ly Agrees to Settle FTC Allegations that It Violated Children's Privacy Law: https://www.ftc.gov/news-events/press-releases/2019/02/

video-social-networking-app-musically-agrees-settle-ftc

- Google and YouTube Will Pay Record $170 Million for Alleged Violations of Children's Privacy Law: https://www.ftc.gov/news-events/press-releases/2019/09/google-youtube-will-pay-record-170-million-alleged-violations

About the Author

DAVID DERIGIOTIS IS A CERTIFIED Information Privacy Professional (CIPP/US) and head of the Professional and Cyber Risk Practice Group with International Wholesale Insurance Broker Burns & Wilcox. David has consulted to the US Department of the Treasury, the Federal Trade Commission surrounding children's online privacy regulation, and has provided cyber and privacy risk insights to the Organization for Economic Co-operation and Development (OECD), an intergovernmental organization made up of thirty-six member countries.

David regularly provides expert commentary for television and radio news outlets concerning data breaches, identity theft, and the various cyber threats facing organizations and individuals. David also serves as a featured speaker and instructor during cybersecurity and risk-management conferences across the country. As a specialist in information-gathering techniques, David routinely provides awareness on the topic of social engineering tactics and discusses the methods used by criminals for establishing a false sense of trust with targets. This unique perspective allows his audience to anticipate attacks and be proactive in their approach to online privacy and cybersecurity. David and his wife have five children and live in the Detroit metropolitan area.